Unlocking Literacy

A Guide for Teachers

Edited by Robert Fisher and Mary Williams

David Fulton Publishers
London

David Fulton Publishers Ltd
Ormond House, 26–27 Boswell Street, London WC1N 3JZ

www.fultonpublishers.co.uk

First published in Great Britain by David Fulton Publishers 2000
Reprinted 2001

Note: The right of Robert Fisher and Mary Williams to be identified as the editors of this work has been asserted by them in accordance with the Copyright, Designs and Patents Act 1988.

British Library Cataloguing in Publication Data

A catalogue record for this book is available from the British Library

ISBN 1–85346–652–2

Typeset by Textype Typesetters, Cambridge
Printed in Great Britain by The Cromwell Press Ltd

Contents

Acknowledgements

We would like to thank the many teachers, student teachers and children in west London schools whose work has informed our research.

We are grateful for permission to include the following published poems and extracts:

'I Saw a Jolly Hunter' and 'My Mother Saw a Dancing Bear' from *Collected Poems* by Charles Causley, published by Macmillan, reprinted by permission of David Higham Associates Limited, 'I'm a Parrot' by Grace Nichols, reproduced with permission of Curtis Brown Group Ltd, on behalf of Grace Nichols, copyright Grace Nichols 1988, and to Nash Pollock Publishing for permission to reproduce material previously published in *First Stories for Thinking* and *First Poems for Thinking* by Robert Fisher.

Every effort has been made to obtain permission to include copyright material in this book; in case of failure to obtain permission the editors and publishers undertake to make good any omissions in future printings.

Notes on contributors

Francoise Allen was first educated in France where she specialised in English Linguistics. She taught languages in multicultural comprehensive schools in west London for ten years, including two years as head of faculty. She is currently course tutor in Modern Foreign Languages in the School of Education at Brunel University and runs the Masters in Secondary Education award. Her research interests include bilingualism and the development of literacy through learning a foreign language.

Robert Catt has taught English within 11–18 comprehensive schools, first in London and then in East Sussex where he was a head of English for ten years. He now teaches professional English at both undergraduate and postgraduate levels including masters and in service education and training (INSET) courses. His interests in language, and talk in particular, have involved research in both the UK and USA. He has recently been an adviser on the reform of teacher education in Poland.

Robert Fisher taught for more than 20 years in primary schools in London and overseas including Ethiopia and Hong Kong, and was a primary headteacher for five years. He has published more than 20 books on aspects of teaching and learning including the *Stories for Thinking* series, *Teaching Thinking: Philosophical Enquiry in the Classroom* and *Head Start: How to Develop your Child's Mind*. He directs the Centre for Research in Teaching Thinking and runs research and development projects for schools and LEAs in developing literacy, thinking and learning.

John Garvey taught for nine years in primary classrooms in London, and was a headteacher of a primary school in Richmond upon Thames. He now teaches in the Brunel School of Education across primary ITT courses with specialisms in Design and Technology and Information and Communication Technology. He is currently award leader for the PGCE Primary Course. His research interests include teaching literacy through the use of Information and Communication Technology. He is the author (with Robert Fisher) of *Investigating Technology* (Simon & Schuster).

Gerry Gregory after National Service in the RAF taught English, history and PE in inner-London comprehensive schools for nine years, and in Brazil for three years, before becoming senior lecturer in English and Education at Shoreditch College of Education (ILEA) in 1971. He joined Brunel University in 1980. He teaches English on Initial Teacher Training courses and supervises research at PhD level. His current research interest is in the teaching of grammar.

Colleen Johnson spent several years as an actor in Canada and the UK, working mainly in theatre in education, cofounding two theatre companies. She has a wide range of teaching experience in primary, secondary, further, adult and higher education, specialising in drama, voice production and lecturing skills. She teaches drama in education at Brunel University and writes and directs plays for community groups and schools. Research interests include the development of the teacher as communicative expert.

Deborah Jones taught in primary schools in London and Cambridgeshire and worked as a member of a language support team. She joined an LEA advisory and inspection service where she worked first on the Language in the National Curriculum (LINC) project and subsequently coordinated assessment for the LEA. She currently teaches on initial teacher training and Masters courses, and pursues research in language education assessment at Brunel University.

Victoria Whitfield completed her PGCE English Training at Brunel University in 1999 and is now a teacher of English at Sunbury Manor School.

Mary Williams worked for 20 years as a primary school teacher, the last nine as headteacher of a nursery/infant school. She lectures on both ITT and Masters courses in language and literacy and teaching English to able children. Research interests include raising standards in literacy at Key Stage 2, an evaluation of the strategies used by able Year 1 pupils as they learn to read and write and metacognition as it relates to English learning. She is subject leader for English within the School of Education of Brunel University.

Introduction

Is there a key somewhere that will help me understand what all these words mean?

(Ben, aged 11)[1]

One of the central purposes of education is to help pupils to read and write. For many children like Ben learning to be literate is a struggle, as they and their teachers search for the key that will unlock the mysteries of learning to read and write. In this book we explore ways to help children like Ben develop their skills in literacy, thinking and learning. We try to show how literacy teaching, including the daily Literacy Hour taught each morning in English schools, can be used creatively and imaginatively to develop reading, writing, speaking and listening with children of all ages and abilities. Drawing on the Brunel Research into Literacy (BRIL) project recently undertaken in west London schools, this book offers a guide for those engaged in teaching literacy and the Literacy Hour in schools, and for all who are interested in improving the quality of reading, writing, speaking and listening of 5–14-year-olds (Key Stages 1–3 in the National Curriculum for England and Wales).

This book is based on a number of underlying beliefs about the benefits that being literate brings. Literacy also brings valuable ways of thinking about ourselves and our world. Being able to read enables us to learn from people we do not and cannot personally know. Written language allows us to communicate across space and time. It gives us access to 'the best that is thought and known in the world'[2]. Learning to be literate is more than learning the basic skills of reading and writing. Access to literature helps to shape the personality, enables us to understand ourselves and others better and develops emotional intelligence[3]. Being literate helps to facilitate critical and creative thinking and the ability to solve problems. Our underlying belief is that reading and writing are not just mechanical skills but are in their most important functions *thinking* activities.

Not all of human thinking needs words, but language is essential for extending thinking, for extending learning through reading and writing and for communicating with others. If words are the tools for thought, as many psychologists such as Vygotsky claim, then teaching children to be literate is to give them tools for thinking[4]. It will enhance children's cognitive growth and help them get more out of learning and of life. As Charlene, aged ten, put it: 'If you did not have words how would you know what to say? How would you know what to think?'

Learning to be literate begins with speaking and listening. Speech enables us to describe the world, but written speech has a separate linguistic function: it enables us to sustain and order our thinking. Writing allows us to reflect on and shape what is said in systematic and sustained ways. Reading enables us to focus on, to make judgements about and to be critical about what we and others have said. As Dean, aged nine, said in explaining the difference between speaking and reading: 'You can go back to a book and see what it says, but once you've said something words fly away and they're gone.'

In this book we have tried to find creative ways of extending children's thinking through their use of language. Language is a social tool used for a wide range of purposes. Our reasons for using language are social, personal and to do with purposes we want to achieve. As Lynette, aged seven, said: 'You have to use words to get what you want.' To help a child become literate means giving them the means to achieve more in learning and in life. Giving children a *purpose* for their reading and writing is another key focus of this book.

Language is the raw material of literature. An aim of literacy teaching is to enable children to experience a wide range of personal, imaginative and functional language. Through literature they learn about the uses of language and the patterns of thought and feeling that language can convey. They learn through literature how the use of language can help create, sustain or destroy relationships. It is through exploring human relationships in literature that moral imagination develops and children acquire, adapt and develop their values. 'You don't understand what it's like until you read about it,' said Joanne, during a class discussion on the value of newspapers. Reading, reflecting on and responding to what is read also provide the essential groundwork for children's own writing[5].

We live in an age of information overload, in a state that the psychologist William James called a 'buzzing, blooming confusion'. How to deal with the welter of information that surrounds us is one of the major challenges our children face in modern society. They must learn not only learn how to cope with information, but how to shape, organise and control it for themselves. The computer and communications technology are sources of endless data. Children need the thinking and information-processing skills that will help them to identify what they need to know, how to access that knowledge, judge its value, interpret and communicate it. They need to be able to answer the question asked by Gary, aged eight, when he was trying to locate information on the computer: 'What do you do once you've got it on the screen?'

Children need to learn through language but also to learn about language. This means learning about the social uses of language as well as the structure of words, sentences and texts. We believe that children's knowledge about language should start from what children can do and from the considerable implicit knowledge about language they already possess. What we suggest in this book are ways of helping them to make this knowledge explicit. Vygotsky argued that there are two stages in the development of literacy: first, its automatic unconscious acquisition (typified when 'natural readers' say they don't know how they learnt to read): and, second active conscious control over their knowledge (such as when a child shapes writing for an audience and a purpose). The term metacognition refers to this conscious control over one's thinking. A theme of this book is to show how children can gain conscious control over the thinking involved in literacy, and how to develop awareness of the nature of language and of themselves as thinkers and learners[6]. We believe that the key to higher order reading and writing skills is higher order thinking. Such thinking is not easy, as Anna, aged ten, said: 'Thinking about thinking is the hardest kind of thinking.' But we believe such thinking, thinking that helps them to gain conscious control of the processes of literacy, is in the grasp of all children if they are given the right kinds of help.

If language is to do with making meaning, we believe that children's literacy is best developed through meaningful activities both in English lessons and elsewhere across the curriculum. These activities need to be structured, but must also be creative so that learning to read and write is seen by children to have real purpose. We offer therefore some models of creative literacy teaching that provide challenge within a structured framework, drawn from the research of our own and others' classroom practice. In particular we focus on the structured framework of the Literacy Hour, now used in schools in England and Wales, and aim to show ways in which teaching in the Literacy Hour can be developed in creative and problem-solving ways to add value, variety and interest to the routines of teaching

In a review of the Literacy Hour undertaken after it had been in operation for two terms the following observations were made by teachers:

- 'It didn't always allow for expressive/creative writing to develop due to the need to keep up pace and vigour.'
- 'There was insufficient time for extended writing.'
- 'Children don't get any time to think . . . I know myself that if I'm composing something, I like some thinking time.'

These perceptions were derived from research into the implementation of the Literacy Hour in which literacy consultants, practising teachers and student teachers were questioned about its strengths and weaknesses[7]. In the following chapters the perceptions of teachers are used to provide the framework for a discussion about current concerns in the teaching and learning of reading and writing. Although we attempt to show how problems can be overcome through creative approaches to teaching, this is not a recipe book. There are many kinds of good teacher, and many ways to teach literacy, and in our view the best ways are those that rely on the critical and reflective judgement of teachers. These judgements need to be underpinned by research and an awareness of what has proved successful and effective in other classrooms, so what we offer here is not only what has worked for us and for our teacher researchers, but what is informed by published research and current initiatives in this country and abroad. Sometimes, as the words of Jody, aged 11, remind us: 'It helps you to think if you hear what others say.'

This book is about the development of language and linguistic intelligence[8] and how to create high quality interaction between teacher and child so as to improve levels of achievement. We aim to show creative ways to teach literacy not only within the Literacy Hour, but beyond it, and to develop critical literacy and higher order reading and writing skills across the curriculum.

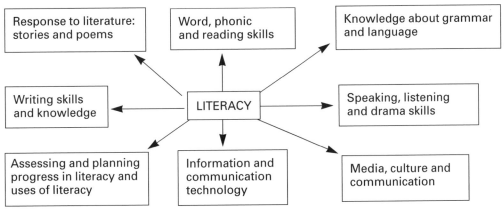

Figure 1: Elements in *Unlocking Literacy*

In this book you will find chapters on the following topics, as pictured in Figure 1:

- Chapter 1: '*Stories are for thinking*' explores ways stories can be used for developing literacy, through questioning and discussion, reading, writing, and other creative activities to help develop thinking across the curriculum. Reading stories is the natural way to unlock and develop the literacy skills of young children. We look at ways of using stories as part of a Literacy Hour lesson, and as a stimulus for thinking with individual children, small groups, whole classes or with larger groups of children, as in a school assembly.

- Chapter 2: '*A poem is alive*' presents ways of using poetry with young children to develop literacy. It shows how children's questions can be a focus for discussing poems within a shared or guided reading session, and how to encourage children to make expressive and creative responses to poems, as well as ideas for composing. This chapter shows how the poetic voice within any child can be unlocked, and how children can be supported in becoming poets themselves.

- Chapter 3: '*Jolly good I said*' presents a rationale for using poetry with older children, and ways of moving children on from familiar and everyday uses of language towards engagement with more demanding language use. The chapter shows how challenging work with children can involve enjoyment, expression and feeling. Dynamic approaches to teaching poetry provide models that can be adapted for use in any classroom to develop literacy and the kinds of interactive and 'intersubjective' teaching that develops higher order thinking and linguistic awareness.

- Chapter 4: '*Playing with words*' presents ways to teach phonic and phonemic awareness, informed by recent research and effective classroom practice. Ideas are given for teaching phonemes with young children and extending phonemic awareness with older children. Other features of work at word level are included here, such as ways of developing vocabulary knowledge and skills in spelling.

- Chapter 5: '*There's only one Michael Owen*' discusses arguments for and against the teaching of grammar. Drawing on research in schools, it presents approaches to teaching grammar within and beyond the Literacy Hour which have been effective in developing children's knowledge about grammar and language. This chapter considers the context of current interest in the teaching and learning of 'grammar' in relation to the National Curriculum and National Literacy Strategy, and argues the case for grammar teaching. It also explores some broad principles and some particular examples of effective grammar teaching and learning.

- Chapter 6: '*Is this write?*' shows how children's writing develops from the early years to a growing control over and awareness of the writing process. It sets out to show how children develop as writers, and how they can be encouraged to write in vigorous, committed, honest and interesting styles, in both narrative and non-narrative forms. A key theme in this chapter is to show how children can learn to match their style to an audience and purpose. Various strategies are suggested to help develop creative approaches to teaching writing in the classroom including how to help pupils gain metacognitive understanding of themselves as writers.

- Chapter 7: '*What did I say?*' focuses on the key roles that speaking and listening play in the development of children's literacy. It shows ways in which these skills can be developed in the classroom and the important role that drama can play in developing not only language skills but also self-esteem, social skills and confidence. Examples of successful classroom work in drama are presented and analysed, showing how drama can be used to enhance learning in English and across the curriculum.

- Chapter 8: '*Where am I going?*' highlights the vital importance of assessing children's progress as well as evaluating the effectiveness of teaching. Included are such questions as: What progress are the children making? How do we assess children's progress, while also teaching them? What should we be doing to assess progress within and beyond the Literacy Hour? This chapter also looks at ways of helping children to assess and set targets for themselves, to raise their self-awareness as readers, writers and users of literacy.
- Chapter 9: '*Incredibly Creative Tools*' presents ways of teaching children to develop literacy through developing their information-handling and ICT skills. The chapter discusses how to help children to access information and how to organise and control it for themselves. It includes ways of helping them identify what they need to know, interpret information and judge its value. In doing so it aims to show not only how ICT can help children enhance their literacy skills, but also how to exercise the critical thinking that is the foundation for citizenship in an 'information age'.
- Chapter 10: '*Media and culture*' explores the links between literacy and culture. It shows ways of developing in children a critical awareness of current media, and how they can be co-creators of our developing literary and social culture. The theme re-emerges of children being not simply passive receivers of information from others but active responders to that information and critical interrogators of texts and of society, so that they learn how to shape words and the future world to their own needs and ends – unlocking literacy for life.

We believe the challenge is to try to retain in our teaching the spirit of the following quotation in the context of the demands of the curriculum:

> Language is a system of sounds, meanings and structures with which we make sense of the world around us. It functions as a tool of thought; as a means of social organisation; as the repository and means of transmission of knowledge; as the raw material of literature, and as the creator and sustainer – or destroyer – of human relationships. It changes inevitably over time and, as change is not uniform, from place to place. Because language is a fundamental part of being human, it is an important aspect of a person's sense of self; because it is a fundamental part of any community, it is an important part of a person's sense of social identity.[9]

This book aims to show how this can be achieved, and how answers may be found to the question, summed up in the words of an eleven-year-old struggling reader: 'Is there a key somewhere that will help me understand what these words mean?'

Notes

1. The quotes from children and examples of classroom teaching presented in this book are drawn from the Brunel Research into Literacy (BRIL) project. The project involved tutors in the English teaching team and student teachers from Brunel University, working in partnership with teachers from local schools in west London.
2. Matthew Arnold (1822–1888) defined the value of literary criticism as 'a disinterested endeavour to learn and propagate the best that is known and thought in the world.' (*The Function of Literary Criticism at the Present Time*).
3. The Bullock Report, *A Language for Life* (DES 1975, p. 124), is eloquent on the value of literature in helping to shape the personality and sharpen critical intelligence, and the importance of literature to learning and life were also echoed in subsequent reports such as the Kingman Report (DES 1988) and Cox Report (DES 1989).
4. Lev Vygotsky (1962) *Thought and Language*. Cambridge, Mass.: MIT Press.

5. The Kingman Report (DES 1988) argued that wide and responsive reading was necessary for children to get an ear for language and a store of ideas for use in writing, and that once expressed through writing these structures would in turn add flexibility and power to children's speech. In this way literacy plays an important role in developing spoken language.
6. For an introduction to metacognition, see Fisher, R. (1998) 'Thinking about thinking: developing metacognition in children', *Early Child Development and Care* **141**, 1–13.
7. Research by Mary Williams, based on teachers' early perceptions of the effectiveness of the literacy hour, revealed concerns about how effective the Literacy Strategy was in developing pupils' writing at Key Stage 2.
8. See *Head Start: How to Develop Your Child's Mind* by Robert Fisher (1999, London: Souvenir Press) for more on the nature of linguistic intelligence and how it can be developed.
9. Cox Report (DES 1989) 6:18.

Chapter 1
'Stories are for thinking': creative ways to share reading

Robert Fisher

Books are not made to be believed, but to be subjected to enquiry. When we consider a book, we must not ask ourselves what it says, but what it means. (Umberto Eco)

What's the point of a story unless you think about it? (Karen, aged 6)

A group of eight-year-old children had been listening to the story of Adam and Eve. 'Was there anything', asked the teacher, 'that was strange, interesting or puzzling about the story?' One child's hand shot up. 'No', said the teacher, the story was a thinking story she wanted them all to stop and think about it. She waited a minute or two while the children thought about the story. She then invited questions. This time many hands shot up. 'How did the snake talk?' 'Why did God create Adam and Eve as adults and not as children?' 'How was the snake bad if everything in the garden was good?' 'Why did God make the snake?' 'When Adam and Eve left the garden where did they go?' 'Did Adam and Eve eat the wild animals?' 'Did the wild animals eat each other?' 'What happened to the Garden of Eden after Adam and Eve left it?' 'Did they know what a child was?' Their questioning and discussion went on for some time. At the end, one of the children said: 'I didn't know there was so much to think about in this story!'

Why stories?

A story is something that might happen to you. (Anne, aged 7)

In every language, and in every culture, story is the fundamental way of organising human experience and understanding the world. The use of stories has long been recognised as a valuable means of developing literacy with children. Stories have the advantage of being embedded in human concerns, yet offer the child the chance to 'decentre' from the immediacy of their personal lives. Stories liberate children from the here-and-now: they are intellectual constructions but they are also life-like. They are intellectually challenging, but also humanly rewarding.

One reason why stories have an affective power is that 'stories have this crucial feature, which life and history lack, that they have beginnings and ends and so can fix meanings to events'[1]. Stories are in a sense 'given' in a way that life, with its messiness and incompleteness, is not. Children live in a mosaic of disconnected bits of experience. Unlike the complexity of everyday events stories have a completeness and an ending. What makes them stories is that their ending completes (in a rational sense) or satisfies (in an affective sense) whatever was introduced at the beginning and elaborated in the middle. As Abigail, aged eight, said: 'In stories you don't know what will happen until the end, but you know you are going to find out.'

A good story creates a possible world as an object of intellectual enquiry. What makes a story challenging is its polysemic nature, the possible layers of meaning and interpretation it contains. A good story draws us in by engaging the emotions. Rahim, aged six, explained this by saying: 'In a good story you never know what is going to happen next'. The fantasy element of stories allows children to reflect more clearly on real experiences through powerful imaginary experience. A story is created to be enjoyed, but if it is a good story it challenges us to interpret and understand it. In listening to stories children learn about the features of narrative, and use of language as well as imagined worlds that move them away from the here and now and engage them in what Coleridge called 'a willing suspension of disbelief'[2]. Recognition of the important role of stories infuses the Framework for Teaching the Literacy Hour, at text, sentence and word level.

Research has shown that children read from a wide range of genres, although adventure stories are the most popular at all ages and for both sexes[3]. The range of reading that children should be introduced to includes:

- traditional stories
- fairy stories
- stories about fantasy worlds
- stories by significant children's authors
- myths, legends and folktales
- fables and animal stories
- adventure stories
- historical stories
- TV adaptations
- stories from a range of cultures.

Children are more likely to develop into thoughtful and critical readers if teachers and parents engage them in discussing what they read. Such discussion is valuable for all children, whatever their age or ability, and is particularly important for boys who are reluctant readers[4].

What is critical literacy?

'I know what the words say but I don't know what they mean,' said a seven-year-old struggling with a difficult book. The first task a reader faces is to find out what the words on the page or screen say. To be a reader one must break the code and decipher what Jamie, aged five, called 'all those funny squiggles, running around like tadpoles on a page'. A reader has first to break the code, decipher the strange marks to answer the question '*What does it say?*' Being able to say the words is not the most important part of reading, but finding out what they mean is. What motivates a reader is the web of meaning woven by the words. If we try to read a book which makes no meaning for us we soon weary of it. Children need to do more than merely say the words if they want to be good at reading: they must understand the many meanings that words convey. If we want them to be active lifelong readers: they will need to think about and develop a critical response to what they read. They need to answer the question '*What does it mean?*'

Critical readers apply creative thinking to their reading. Helping children to be critical readers means helping them to be more than readers of the plot. They need to be able to interpret the story, to read the lines, but also to read between the lines and beyond the lines. They need the skills to be able to question, rethink and develop their ideas and understanding of what they read. We want them to discover that the reading is not over when a story is finished, but continues through reflection, inferences and deductions, through translating ideas into their own words and making their own interpretations of what they read. We want them to be able to make a personal response to the story, to answers the question: *'What does it mean to me?'* This is a creative act for no story or text will be responded to in quite the same same by any two readers.

If children are to become critical readers in the fullest sense they also need to be reading-users, and to answer the question: *'What can we do with it?'* Critical readers are able to recreate and respond to texts, and also to use them for their own creative purposes. Any story can be a stimulus for a child's own story-writing (for more on developing story-writing see Chapter 6).

A reader is not the 'author' of the text, as some theorists have claimed, any more than a pianist playing Mozart is the composer. But a reader, like a musician, is engaged in an act of interpretation which is also an act of self-expression. A piece of music can be played or a story read at a literal level by simply playing the notes or reading the words. But at a deeper level we understand the story (or music) by linking it to our own experience of life. This provides the deeper pleasures in reading, and explains why a good story or book can be returned to again and again. As Tracy, aged eight, put it: 'A good story makes you think how would you feel if it happened to you.'

Interrogating the text

'A good story is adventure,' said Ben, aged six. It is an adventure for the characters involved, but is also an adventure in thinking. It invites the reader to make a leap of imagination. Children need to be helped to make the imaginative leap that expands their thinking. One way of doing this is through questioning. By asking questions, teachers model what good readers do as they try to make sense of what they read. We ask the questions we hope our children will later learn to ask themselves. Such questions help develop the habits of mind of good readers. They practise with us what they will later do by themselves. So what kinds of question should we be asking?

A story has a setting, so one question we can always ask is *'What kind of world is this?'* All stories occur in a place and at some time. Part of the adventure of a story is to be taken on a magic carpet of the mind to other places and other times, to meet other people doing things that might be very similar or very different to what we do. Any story can be explored by asking questions such as those in Figure 1.1.

After reading or hearing the story the first challenge which can be presented to a young child is to ask them to recollect and retell the events of the story in their own words. Young children are, of course, very keen to tell a story in the right way, in the right order. As Lucy, aged five, said after hearing some deviation in the retelling of the Cinderella story: 'That's not the right story. You have got to tell it right.'

Once the story is established in their minds, children can enjoy playing with the narrative if they are encouraged to do so. An example of this occurred when Rumpelstiltskin was being used as a story for thinking with five-year-olds. Once the story had been read, reconstructed and discussed some of the children were invited to act out their own version in front of the class. They volunteered to play the different parts and with a few props began acting the story. The child playing the king rode into the village and listened to the mother in the story say how her daughter could spin straw into gold. The king then asked whether the daughter would go with him to the palace to do just that. The mother thought about this request and then said: 'No'. The

Key aspect	Some questions to ask
• *Setting*	When is it (now or a long time ago)? Where is it (here or somewhere else)? What is it like there (how is it like/unlike here)?
• *Character*	Who are the characters in the story (can you name them)? How would you describe them (what do they look like)? How are the characters related?
• *Plot*	What happens in the story? What was/were the key events? What might have happened?
• *Point of view*	What does the character think? What do the other characters think? What do you think?
• *Dialogue*	What did the character(s) say? Why did they say that? What might they have said?
• *Language*	What special words are there (what new words)? What sound/spelling patterns can you see? What punctuation is used? why?
• *Themes*	What is the story about? What is strange, interesting or puzzling about the story? What questions or comments do you have about the story?

Figure 1.1: Questions to extend children's thinking about a story

king asked again, the daughter said she would go but the mother refused. The king tried once more but again the mother said no, her daughter could not go with the king, she must stay at home. So the king, not knowing what to do, rode away and that was the end of their version of the story. Afterwards, the girl who played the mother was asked why she had not followed the usual storyline and allowed the king to take her daughter to the palace. She replied: 'Because I knew what would happen if he did!' (For more on developing literacy through drama see Chapter 7.)

Another kind of personal response is to try to visualise the setting, characters or events in the story and some children, like adults, are better at seeing with their 'mind's eye' than others. Visual thinking is an important means of learning, remembering and coming to know things. We are all to some extent visual learners. Some children learn best through exercising their visual intelligence[5]. This capacity can be stimulated by asking them to close their eyes and to visualise the story they are reading or hearing in their 'mind's eye', or by taking them for a walk through an imagined scene which you describe while they try to visualise what it looks like. Talk afterwards about what they could see or not see. One child reported after a visualisation session: 'It's like you've got a tele inside your head,' but another responded: 'The trouble is I don't know how to switch mine on.'

A story is made meaningful by linking it to personal experience, and by identifying with the characters. If you were a character in the story, who would you want to be? Why? What would you do, say, think and feel? When a group of six-year-olds was asked which character in the story of Cinderella they would like to be, one child replied: 'A mouse' (the sort that was changed into a horse to pull Cinderella's carriage).

When asked why, he said: 'Because I like cheese, and so does a mouse.'

Young children often find it difficult to articulate a personal response to a story. As Melanie, aged seven, said: 'It's hard to say what you mean.' But although what they say can seem incoherent, their insights may contain the seeds of a more sophisticated understanding. They often have in their minds more than they can say. Our challenge is to help them to develop and express their intellect: to think for themselves, give voice to their ideas, form their own judgements and personal insights, and take pride in having a personal point of view.

One method for achieving this, which has been used successfully across the world, is that of Philosophy for Children. This is a method of using a story as a stimulus for creating what is called a 'community of enquiry' with any group of children[6]. Before looking at ways of using stories in a community of enquiry, as part of a Literacy Hour, we will discuss the kinds of higher order reading skills that can be developed using a 'Stories for Thinking' approach.

Developing higher order reading skills

> Oh I get it, we're not supposed to read the story, we are supposed to think about it.
>
> (James, aged 7)

Once children are able to 'crack' the language code, through being able to read and write at a basic level, they will need to practise their reading with challenging texts and develop the higher order skills that will enable them extend and improve their standard of reading. The following are some of the higher order reading skills that they need to develop:

- skimming
- scanning
- reflective reading: questioning, analysing, predicting
- reasoning: making inferences, deductions and connections
- evaluating.

Skimming is the ability to get the overall gist of a text and to gather the main points. Asking the child to skim through the story before or after you have read it and then to reconstruct it provides practise in skimming. The ability to skim a story or book is important for finding out quickly what the writing is about. This can be done at a superficial level, like Woody Allen who, when asked what Tolstoy's *War and Peace* was about, said 'Russia', or the child when asked to summarise the story 'Puss in Boots' said: 'a cat'. The value of the use of short stories in the Literacy Hour is that skimming can be carried out relatively easily by both teacher and child. Play the 'Skim a Story' game: speedily skim a story then look away and see how quickly (and accurately) you can tell what the story is about or recall it. Try getting children to practise their skimming skills by this method.

Scanning means looking rapidly but intensely at a text to identify a particular part; for example, the name of a character or when a particular event occurred. Questions to encourage children to scan the text actively include: 'Can you find the part in the story where . . . ?' or, if children are referring to the story: 'Show me where in the story it says . . .' Play games such as 'Hunt the Word' to help develop their scanning skills by asking them to scan the story to find a particular word, sentence or punctuation mark.

Reflective reading means making a thoughtful response to texts: for example, by questioning or analysing what or why something has happened or by making predictions about what is being read. This is important if children are to learn from what they read. Like all skills it develops best when it is practised. A child will learn to question, analyse and make hypotheses about what might happen next by seeing others do it and then doing it themselves. Any text that is read is there to be analysed and questioned. When asked how many questions could be asked about a story, one seven-year-old, who was practised in the art of enquiry, replied: 'More than any of us can think of. You can never run out of questions, because there is always another possible question.'

Reasoning involves making inferences and deductions from text. The trouble with language is that words are not the objects they describe and represent but are all in a sense metaphoric. They stand for things, but are not the things themselves and so must always be somehow incomplete. The words 'old woman', for example, might refer to any one of a number of old women, who might be a range of ages or even of different genders! So it is always possible to ask: 'Who is this old woman?' or 'What is she like?' and draw inferences from clues in the text to help answer the question more fully. Inferences involve using reasons or evidence to reach a conclusion which is more or less likely to be true. During the discussion of one story a child suggested that the woman in the story might be a man dressed up as a woman. This was, of course, possible but the children decided that this was unlikely for there was no evidence in the story to support it. 'What man would want to dress up as a woman?' asked Darren (a question it was decided to leave for another time).

Deductions are inferences from text using reasoning alone. For example, any character referred to as 'she' must be female. This is true by definition, as are other things about her: for instance, if she is a person, then one day she was born and one day she will die. If all humans are mortal and Cinderella is human, then Cinderella must be mortal. A great deal can be deduced from the meanings of words, which is why getting children to explain and define them is so important. 'It depends what you mean by. . .' is a frequent question posed by philosophers for they know that many arguments and misunderstandings in life arise because people interpret the meanings of words differently. Inferences and deductions from stories are made by exploring what the words of the story imply. As Jade, aged five, said, puzzling over a word she did not understand: 'If I knew what the word meant I'd know the story.'

To be a critical reader more is needed than just knowing the tale. A story can be evaluated by being compared with others which means assessing the story critically: for example, by judging what we like or do not like about it and by establishing what is good or bad about it. One way to evaluate a story is to compare it with others that have already been read. Every good story:

● has an author (or number of authors)	Who is telling this story?
● is a special kind of story (genre)	What kind of story is this?
● can be linked to other stories	Is this story like another story you know? How?
● is special (or original in some way)	What is noteworthy about this story?

Developing moral judgement

A child once said to me (getting her words in the wrong order): 'Every moral has a story'. All stories have a moral dimension if they concern aspects of human behaviour. It is often easier to understand fictional situations than situations in our own lives because we can view stories about others from a distanced and more dispassionate viewpoint. The challenging aspects of life are less threatening in stories than in real life. Stories are therefore an excellent vehicle for discussing moral issues, initiating children into thinking about meanings and values, through asking questions such as:

● How are people (characters) behaving in the story?
● How should they behave?
● How would you behave if you were them?

Other questions which can be used to explore the moral dimensions of any story include:

Key question	*Moral dimension*
● 'Have we thought of. . . ?'	Imagination
● 'How would you feel if. . . ?'	Empathy
● 'What if everybody did . . . ?'	Making a principle universal
● 'What would happen if . . . ?'	Anticipating consequences
● 'What alternatives are there . . . ?'	Hypothetical reasoning
● 'Is it a good reason . . . ?'	Giving good reasons
● 'Is this the sort of person you want to be?'	Projecting an ideal self
● 'Is this the sort of world you'd like to live in?'	Projecting an ideal world

One way to involve children in the exercise of literary and moral judgement through shared reading is by creating a community of enquiry in the classroom. A community of enquiry teaches by example, enabling children to practise both a critical approach to reading and to develop habits of rational behaviour through the experience of being in a group where being reasonable (that is giving reasons for what you say and do) and listening to others are the norm. By encouraging children to think, reason and to make moral judgements about the behaviour of others, they are likely to be more considerate, more reasonable and thoughtful about their own behaviour. Literature can be a moral force that will help educate a child's mind and emotions. As Liane, aged seven, said, in summing up what she learnt from the shared discussion of a story: 'You should always stop and think first.'

Creating a community of enquiry

You should listen to other people because sometimes they have good ideas. (Jamie, aged 6)

A community of enquiry occurs where reading is shared in a group and discussed in a safe and stimulating environment, that is, a place where children learn to think for themselves and to value the thinking of others. The first task in a community of enquiry is to make children feel comfortable, secure and at ease with their teacher and with each other. Ideally, adult and children should be sitting at the same level, on the floor or on chairs in a circle or horseshoe shape, so that all can see, hear and talk to each other easily. This may not be possible but even so a sense of community can be achieved in a setting which is not ideal. To overcome the problem of having her session interrupted by visitors one teacher put a sign outside her class saying: 'Do not disturb, thinking in progress.'

In a community of enquiry or thinking circle the teacher takes responsibility for creating the form of the discussion, but the *content* should be as far as possible the responsibility of the children. As with any discussion, certain ground rules may need to be established beforehand, or written up for all to see. Some examples are: 'we take turns', 'we speak one at a time', 'we listen to each other', and 'we respect what people say'. It can be helpful to begin by playing a thinking game that embodies the rules and encourages children to listen carefully to each other[7].

A community of enquiry invites children into the club of critical readers. Children who engage in a community of enquiry acquire habits which reflect their experience in the community. If they listen to each other, express their own opinions, and build on each other's ideas they will grow into adults who are willing to listen, who are confident in saying what they think and who are thoughtful about what others say. They will acquire self-esteem about themselves as thinkers and readers.

In a typical community of enquiry the teacher will:

- read the story
- invite comments or questions
- lead a discussion
- invite children to review the discussion
- introduce further group or individual activity.

This is how these elements apply to a Stories for Thinking lesson:

1. Reading the story

If the children are non-readers the teacher will read the story or text. It is helpful with young children to read the story twice. The second time is a 'thinking time', when, as they listen, the children are asked to think about anything that might be strange, interesting or puzzling about the story. Children who are readers take turns in reading part of the story, for example, a paragraph each. Any children in the group who cannot read or who find reading very difficult say 'pass' and the next child continues the reading.

2. Inviting comments or questions

   I have a lot of questions that I haven't yet thought of. (Cassie, aged 7)

After the story has been read by teacher and children, it is time to think about it. Allow some quiet thinking time then ask the children if there is anything strange, interesting or puzzling about the story. Prevent quick children (the 'hare brains' in the group) from shouting out the first thing they think of by saying you are going to give everyone time to think. Thinking time encourages more thoughtful responses, and allows time for more elaborate thinking and for children to formulate questions.

Once the children have had time to think, ask for their comments or questions and write each one in the child's words on the board. Add the child's name after his or her comment or question to acknowledge each contribution. You may need to help children formulate their comment into a question or to express their thoughts fully. Try as much as possible to use the child's own words, and check with them that the changes you propose are what they want to say – as in the following excerpt from a discussion:

Child: He was a bad man.
Teacher: We could turn that into a question, couldn't we – Was he a bad man? or Why was he a bad man?
Child: Why was he a bad man? (Teacher now writes this up as a question.)

Once you have a number of questions or comments on the board, each linked to the name of one or more children (for several children might have the same thought or idea) you will have a number of responses to the story to explore in discussion.

Choose one of the questions, or ask the children to choose one, by voting which they would like to discuss. When the question has been selected begin the discussion by asking the child whose question it is to say why they asked it, and invite others to respond to what is said.

One advantage of writing questions on a chart is that you have a record of contributions that can be added to later or compared with other lists. A frequent finding is that the more experienced children get at interrogating texts the better at it they become. As one teacher reported: 'For the first few stories the children gave few comments or questions, after six weeks I got twice as many, and now [after a term] they often ask more questions than I can fit onto the board.' Of her lists of questions another teacher said: 'It provides me with written evidence that this is an enquiring classroom.'

3. Leading a discussion

> I like it when we have a 'thinking time' about stories. (Sonal, aged 6)

One way to facilitate the discussion is to ask who agrees or disagrees with particular comments that have been made. The teacher should aim to lead but not to dominate the discussion. Initially you will need to ask a lot of questions yourself particularly the key question: 'Why?' As the group gets better at discussing together the balance of teacher and pupil participation will change and as the community develops the children should do more of the speaking. As Jemma, aged eight, said: 'A story circle is different because it is our turn to say what we think.'

Using a story for thinking

The story on page 10 is appropriate for 5–8-year-olds. Use the questions below to stimulate their thinking about it and a key theme from it[8].

To aid discussion there are two kinds of questions which can be asked about the story: They involve children in reading the lines and 'reading between the lines'. First ask questions that challenge children's thinking at the literal level of the story, by probing their knowledge of and ability to draw inferences from the text. The examples listed below show the kinds of questions you could ask to elicit an understanding of the main features of the story.

Thinking about the story

Key question: What does the story mean?
- How many cats were there? How do you know?
- What did the cats find?
- What is a chapatti?
- Where was the chapatti? Why was it there?
- Why did the cats quarrel?
- Why did the monkey want the chapatti?
- What was the monkey's plan to get the chapatti for himself?
- When did the cats realise they had been tricked?
- Do you think the monkey was right when he said the last piece was too small to cut in half?
- What do you think the moral of this story is?

The Cats and the Chapatti

Once upon a time two cats found a chapatti. A chapatti is a kind of Indian bread, a little like a flat pancake. The cats were greedy and began to quarrel over it.

'It's mine!' said one cat. 'I saw it first!'

'No, it's mine,' said the other cat. 'I saw it before you!'

While the cats were arguing a monkey came by and he looked at the chapatti. He felt hungry and wanted the chapatti for himself.

The monkey thought for a while, then said, 'Sisters, why are you quarrelling? To be fair you should share the chapatti and split it in two. Let me break it in half for you.'

At first the cats were not sure. Was this a fair thing to do? They soon agreed it was. So the monkey picked up the chapatti and broke it into two pieces. He then held the pieces up for the cats to see.

'Oh dear,' he said, 'look, one piece is larger than the other,' and he broke a bit off the larger piece and ate it. He held the pieces up again.

'Oh dear,' he said, 'they are still not equal,' and he broke off another piece and popped it in his mouth. The two cats watched, not realising what was happening.

Again, the monkey held the pieces up and said, 'Oh dear, they are *still* not equal', and ate another piece off the bigger bit. The clever monkey carried on doing this and the pieces became smaller and smaller. Still the cats could not see his plan.

At last there was only one small piece left. 'Oh dear,' he said, 'it's too small to cut in half,' so he quickly gobbled it up and ran away laughing. The two cats stared at each other and slowly realised that they had been tricked by the clever monkey.

Questions should not be limited to the literal level. We should try, as Vygotsky said, to move children on to more abstract and conceptual modes of thinking[9]. The second kind of questions are at a conceptual rather than literal level and probe a child's personal understanding of a theme or concept drawn from the story. They are about reading beyond the lines and seek a personal response to an issue in the story. They are open questions that encourage children to consider a variety of viewpoints, ideas and arguments, rather than seeking one right answer. They are not about trying to 'guess what is in the teacher's head'. They are trying to get children to think for themselves.

The following list gives the kinds of question which could be asked about one theme from the story.

Thinking about quarrelling

Key question: What is a quarrel?
- What does it mean to quarrel with someone?
- Why do people quarrel? What reasons are there for quarrels?
- How many people are there in a quarrel?
- Can you quarrel with yourself? Have you ever had a quarrel with yourself?
- Have you ever had a quarrel with other people? Give an example.
- Do you only quarrel with someone you don't like?
- What do you do if your friends start quarrelling?
- How could you help them end a quarrel?
- What is the best way of keeping out of quarrels?
- Is it ever good to have a quarrel? Why or why not?

The questions above only model the kind that might stimulate thinking and discussion.

By planning possible questions which are appropriate and challenging for your children beforehand you will always have something to ask if the discussion flags, and by so doing you will model for the child the intelligent habits of an enquiring reader. But the most important questions are those raised by the children themselves.

The following is part of a discussion with six- and seven-year-old children (Year 2) after they had read 'The Cats and the Chapatti'. They had chosen to answer Anna's question about the story: 'Why did they quarrel?'

Child:	There were some animals quarrelling.
Teacher:	What were they saying?
Child:	'No you can't', 'Yes you can' . . . that sort of thing.
Child:	They were contradicting each other.
Teacher:	So a quarrel is like a contradiction?
Child:	. . . (after a pause for thought) Yes.
Child:	They were quarrelling with each other.
Teacher:	Can you quarrel with yourself?
Child:	You can't quarrel with yourself. You need to have more than one person.
Child:	You can quarrel with yourself. You could punch yourself. Your brain quarrels with you . . . if you want to test yourself.
Child:	I disagree with Sarah. You can't quarrel with yourself. You haven't done anything to yourself.
Child:	If you punch your leg, it can't say 'No'. Your brain says 'No'.
Teacher:	Can animals say 'Yes' and 'No'?
Child:	No, only people can say 'Yes' and 'No'. That's how we are different from animals.

At the end of the discussion the children were asked to talk about the story in groups and to report back what they thought was its moral. Here are some of their replies:

- Don't trust anyone. (James)
- Don't fight and quarrel. (Andrew)
- Don't be greedy or someone may take what you've got. (Ryan)
- Share with other people. (Conor)
- Don't fight or quarrel with your friends. (Sarah)
- Be kind to everyone. (Emily)

In the early stages of a community of enquiry, discussions tend to be totally teacher directed, but the aim is to shift the focus away from yourself so that the children will, through working together, become able to take more responsibility for the discussion and for the way the community of enquiry functions. Try to encourage this, once the children are familiar with the process, by asking them to respond to each other and to look at the person to whom they are responding and not at you. Introduce the convention 'I agree with. . .' or 'I disagree with . . .' and get the children to say with whom they are agreeing or disagreeing. Sometimes invite the child who has spoken to nominate the next speaker, if there is more than one other who wishes to speak.

A number of questions have been found useful for injecting intellectual rigour into a discussion with young children. They aim to move it away from a situation where children simply give an answer with an anecdotal comment or unsupported observations to a style of discussion characterised by the giving of reasons and the formulation of argument. They try to encourage children to take responsibility for their comments and to think about what they are saying. The hope is that such questions, in time, will become internalised and come to be asked by the children themselves.

Examples of questions found useful in discussions include:

Questions	Cognitive function of questions
• What do you think . . . (giving child's name)? What is your view/opinion/idea about this?	*Focusing attention*
• Why do you say that? Can you give me a reason?	*Reasoning*
• What do you mean by . . . ? Can anyone explain that to us?	*Defining/analysing/clarifying*
• Has anyone got another thought/ idea/example? Who else can say something about it?	*Generating alternative views*
• How could we tell if it was true? How do you/we know?	*Testing for truth*
• Who agrees/disagrees with . . . (child's name)? Why? Can you say who/what you agree or disagree with?	*Sustaining dialogue/argument*
• Who can remember what we have said? What are the ideas/arguments we have put forward? Which ideas were good?	*Summarising*

Teachers could expect to see evidence of progress after a number of such sessions. The sorts of evidence teachers report include an improvement in the children's abilities under the headings displayed in the box below:

Evidence: *children can:*	Skills: *children show:*
• listen to each other	listening skills
• formulate and ask questions	questioning and enquiry skills
• think of good/new ideas	creative thinking
• translate their thoughts and ideas into words	communication
• communicate their ideas	speaking skills
• respond to others in a discussion	cooperative and social skills
• give reasons for what they think	verbal reasoning skills
• develop their understanding of challenging concepts	concept building
• read and respond critically to texts	critical reading skills

(For more on assessing children's progress in literacy see Chapter 8.)

The community of enquiry provides the opportunity for systematic, sustained and supportive discussion of texts. The teacher helps pupils to assume responsibility for their own ideas, to think for themselves and to benefit from the suggestions, hypotheses and insights of others. By participating in a community founded on reasoning, freedom of expression and mutual respect the children will experience what it means to be a free citizen in a democracy, with the freedom to question, to challenge and to exercise personal choice. There is no better preparation for being an active citizen in such a country than for a child to participate with others in a community of enquiry. In learning how to interrogate texts they will also be developing the skills and confidence to interrogate all aspects of their world. (For more on links between culture and literacy see Chapter 10.)

Stories for Thinking and the Literacy Hour

> The teacher demonstrates reading strategies with a shared text. The class reads the text together and discusses ideas and textual features, engaging in a high level of interaction with the teacher. (National Literacy Strategy definition of shared reading, DfEE 1998)

> When we are talking about stories I like to have enough time to do it. (Kate, aged 6)

During shared reading in the Literacy Hour the teacher demonstrates reading strategies using a shared text. As in a community of enquiry the class reads the story together, discusses ideas and textual features, engaging in a high level of interaction with the teacher. The aim is to engage all children in the sorts of thoughtful reading habits that are characteristic of good readers. Research has found that 'poor readers are not nearly adept as older children and good readers, respectively, in engaging in planful activities either to make cognitive progress or to monitor it.'[10]. The Stories for Thinking method can add value to a Literacy Hour through its planned approach to pupil questioning, reasoning and critical thinking about texts. Some of the similarities and differences between a Stories for Thinking/community of enquiry approach and the Literacy Hour as outlined in the National Literacy Strategy (DfEE 1998) are shown below:

A Literacy Hour aims to develop:	Stories for Thinking aims to develop:
literacy: reading, writing, speaking and listening	literacy: critical and creative thinking, questioning and reasoning as well as reading, writing, speaking and listening
reading and reflecting at text level, with emphasis on teacher questioning	reading and reflecting on text, with emphasis on pupil questioning
sentence level work to improve comprehension and composition	sentence level work in creating questions and comments
word level work to improve phonics, spelling and vocabulary	word level work in defining meanings of words and developing concepts
a plenary session for sharing and reviewing work.	review of the discussion, as well as review of work.

The Literacy Hour and Stories for Thinking share some common features. Both emphasise the importance of discussing the text to identify themes, ideas, and implicit meanings. Both aim to develop critical reading skills. Stories for Thinking emphasises the importance of children formulating their own questions and aims to add philosophical depth to the discussion. Stories are of course not the only source of literary stimulus for thinking: poetry and information texts can also be used. The Literacy Hour emphasises the importance of work at word level and sentence level as well as at text level[11].

Many teachers are exercising their professional judgement in adapting the Literacy Hour to benefit from a Stories for Thinking approach. Others prefer to find time, usually once a week, for more extended story discussion than the Literacy Hour allows. Stories for Thinking offers a flexible model which can be used in ways which suit the teacher and the children. It will develop literacy but is about more than that: it is also about teaching children to think, in particular to think philosophically about stories and about themselves and the world.

A Stories for Thinking lesson may have different names, such as Thinking Circle, Literacy Hour or even Philosophy for Children. Whatever it is called, children are often quick to see the value of having time set aside to think about and through stories. Kirandeep, aged eight, says such discussions are important because 'thinking is what we are here for'. Karen, aged eight, says she likes Stories for Thinking lessons because they makes stories 'a kind of puzzle'. This puzzling quest, once begun, can lead to a lifelong absorption in reading and making meaning from stories.

Notes

1. Kieran Egan (1986) *Teaching as Story Telling*. London: Methuen.
2. 'That willing suspension of disbelief for the moment, which constitutes poetic faith.' (Coleridge 1827, *Biographia Literaria*, Ch. 14).
3. For more on children's reading choices see M. Coles and C. Hall (1999) *Children's Reading Choices*. London: Routledge.
4. For a discussion of research into boys' underachievement in reading, see E. Millard (1997) *Differently Literate: Boys, Girls and the Schooling of Literacy*. London: Falmer Press.
5. See R. Fisher (1999b) *Head Start: How to Develop Your Child's Mind* (Souvenir Press) for a discussion of a children's multiple intelligences, including visual intelligence, and ways of developing them.
6. See R. Fisher (1998) *Teaching Thinking: Philosophical Enquiry in the Classroom* (Cassell) for an introduction to the theory and practice of philosophy with children. For further information contact: SAPERE (Society for the Advancement of Philosophical Enquiry and Reflection in Education), Web site: www.ndirect.co.uk/~sapere/.
7. See R. Fisher (1997) *Games for Thinking*. Oxford: Nash Pollock for some thinking games.
8. The story and questions appear in *First Stories for Thinking* by R. Fisher (1999a, Nash Pollock), p. 56.
9. Lev Vygotsky argued that if you limit learners to literal or 'concrete' thinking you 'suppress the rudiments of abstract thought such children have . . . school should make every effort to push them to develop in them what is intrinsically lacking in their own development'. 1978. Cambridge, Mass: Harvard University Press. L. Vygotsky *Mind in Society*, p. 89.
10. R. Garner (1987) *Metacognition and Reading Comprehension*. Norwood, New Jersey: Ablex.
11. See *The National Literacy Strategy: Framework for Teaching*. (DfEE 1998) for more on the importance of text, sentence and word level work with texts.

Further reading

Coles, M. and Hall, C. (1999) *Children's Reading Choices*. London: Routledge.
DfEE (1998) *The National Literacy Strategy: Framework for Teaching*. London: HMSO.
Egan, K. (1986) *Teaching as Story Telling*. London: Methuen.
Fisher, R. (1996) *Stories for Thinking*. Oxford: Nash Pollock.
Fisher, R. (1997) *Poems for Thinking*. Oxford: Nash Pollock.
Fisher, R. (1998) *Teaching Thinking: Philosophical Enquiry in the Classroom*. London: Cassell.
Fisher, R. (1999a) *First Stories for Thinking*. Oxford: Nash Pollock.
Fisher, R. (1999b) *Head Start : How to Develop Your Child's Mind*. London: Souvenir Press.
Fisher, R. (2000) *First Poems for Thinking*. Oxford: Nash Pollock.
Millard, E. (1997) *Differently Literate: Boys, Girls and the Schooling of Literacy*. London: Falmer Press.

Chapter 2
'A poem is alive': using poetry with young children

Robert Fisher

Poetry comes from playing the best game of words which has ever been invented.
(Geoffrey Grigson)[1]

Poems say things better than you can. (Sarah, aged 7)

Every child is born with the poetic ability to respond to words and ideas in a playful way. From their earliest days young children respond and revel in verbal play through the syllabic rhythm of first words such as 'ma-ma' or 'da-da-da-da'. The babbling speech of a young child is an early expression of the poetic capacity to play with sounds. As they grow older, children will use words to play with ideas, like the three-year-old who said one autumn: 'Look, the tree is snowing leaves.'

Poetry begins with a fascination for words and with enjoyment of word games. The following example of rhyming words were strung together by a group of four-year-olds: 'sad dad had a bad lad', 'may play today stay' and 'vet in a jet sent me a wet pet'. How do we build on this early wordplay with rhymes and rhythms and extend it to an enjoyment and understanding of poetry?

Poetry begins by feeding the ear. Children like to listen to poems. They delight in word-sounds and wordplay. They will read old favourites over and over again and enjoy learning a favourite poem by heart. Children have a natural ear for rhyme and rhythm, and poetry feeds this innate response to the patterns of spoken language. The love of poetry begins in the delight of shared wordplay[2]. The gift of words, wrapped in riddles, rhymes and poetry is an enduring gift. 'A poem is', as Anne, aged ten, says, 'like a present in words.'

Research shows that a rich diet of nursery rhymes is an important factor in subsequent success in learning to read[3]. Children's experience of rhyme and rhythm should be extended to an enjoyment of poetry, to appreciate how it sounds, what it says and the ways it uses language for literary effect. The Framework for teaching the Literacy Hour lays stress on the interplay of listening to, reading and writing poetry. It encourages teachers to share a range of poetry with children, including:

- informal wordplay and word games
- action rhymes and chants
- nursery and traditional rhymes
- poems by significant children's authors
- riddles, tongue-twisters and shape poems.

Our task as teachers is to help children move on from a love of simple rhyme to an appreciation of poetry that will feed the eye and mind as well as the ear. Both understanding and enjoyment are needed to fully appreciate a poem⁴. A poem is written to contain a distilled essence of meaning, what Ted Hughes (1967) calls the 'spirit' of the poem. As Hughes says the meaning or spirit of a poem is made up of its living parts, its words, images and rhythms. Helping children to discover the spirit and to make sense of a poem can be one of the most rewarding aspects of teaching English. Teaching then becomes a shared literary adventure when children and teacher meet to enjoy and understand better what is written. 'I don't like poems I don't understand', says Henry, aged six, 'so you need someone to read with you.'

The secret of introducing children to poetry is simple. Like learning a language the best way is immersion. Simply plunge in and share the poetry you like with children and do it often. Teaching poetry turns out to be simpler once one is doing it. 'A poem a day' is an uncomplicated recipe, but reading just one poem a day to a class or a child will create a rich resource of language experience (see Figure 2.1). Giving children a varied range of poetry books to look at and discuss and asking them to choose their favourites to have read out will help begin that process of learning to be discerning readers, writers, listeners and speakers.

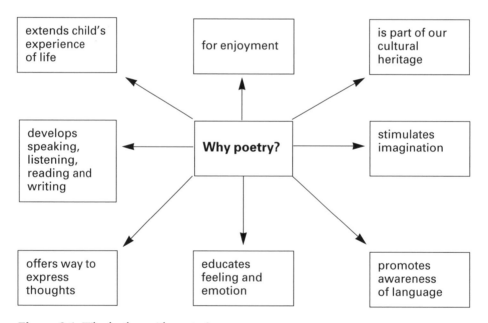

Figure 2.1: Why bother with poetry?

What young children need is a rich range of poetry to read and to hear. Hearing particular poems and rhymes a number of times will help them internalise the words and sounds, and they will begin to memorise spontaneously their favourite rhymes. What parents and teachers can do is to help children both to hear and to understand poems. They can explain what to expect from a poem or poetry book, help them through questioning and discussion to make meaning from poems, and show them how they too can communicate through poetry and help them to create their own poems. But what is a poem?

It takes time to absorb a poem, to explore the world it creates, its language, its sounds and the message or story it conveys. Dylan Thomas once said poetry 'makes you laugh, cry, prickle, be silent, makes your toenails twinkle'. The purposes of poetry are wider than any other kind of writing; poems can be used to tell stories, play games with language, record experience, or reflect thoughts and feelings. A poem might be about the real world or an invented world of the imagination. Or both. A poem can transform the ordinary into the extraordinary. It can give voice to an inner world of dreams and imaginings. Like philosophy, poetry often begins in wonder about the world, and the ways in which words can reflect, distort and transform the world. As Theseus says in Shakespeare's *A Midsummer Night's Dream*[5]:

> The poet's eye in a fine frenzy rolling,
> Doth glance from heaven to earth, from earth to heaven;
> And as imagination bodes forth
> The forms of things unknown, the poet's pen
> Turns them into shapes, and gives to airy nothing
> A local habitation and a name.

Every poem is about something, and uses words in a special way. It uses 'the best words in the best order' as Coleridge said[6], to tell its story.

How can children be helped to respond to poetry? A poem may lead to many kinds of thoughts, feelings and ideas. There is no one way but many to experience or appreciate a poem and some ways of using poems to help young children enjoy poetry and become more able readers will now be explored. The literary roles we seek to develop through poetry can be summed up as code-breaker, meaning-maker, reading-responder and reading-user and each role is associated with a key question that can be asked about any poem (see below):

Ways of working with a poem	*Roles of the child*	*Key questions*
• Speaking and listening • Reading	Code-breaker	What does it say?
• Questionioning • Discussing	Meaning-maker	What does it mean?
• Expressing	Reading-responder	What does it mean to me?
• Composing	Reading-user	What can we do with it?

We will now look more closely at these ways of working with poetry.

Speaking and listening

Poetry is made for speaking. The earliest poetry was spoken or sung. The first poems that children hear are often the half-remembered nursery rhymes recited to them by parents. These early rhymes may be much repeated, and there is good reason for this. According to the poet W. H. Auden, what makes a poem special is that it is 'memorable speech'[7]. A poem lays down a track in the memory that can be travelled over again and again, so that language becomes embedded in experience. The words and phrases of a much-loved poem or nursery rhyme become not merely items of knowledge, but are given life and meaning by being embedded in an original poem which becomes part of us when laid down in long-term memory. When learning by heart in the natural way, through repeated opportunities to speak and listen, children are connected to their literary inheritance. When they share the words and thoughts of a poem, they are given a poetic voice through which to speak, and words which will echo in the memory. Later, having listened to and expressed the voices of others, they will come to create poetry using their own words and ideas.

A love of poetry begins with listening. Lucky the child who has poetry read to them each week by a parent or teacher. Some teachers try to read a poem a day to their class, with maybe a 'favourite poem' session on Friday. Children can also be encouraged to listen on their own, or with others, to poetry tapes. Listening to poems can become a regular part of classroom activity. A section of the classroom can be turned into a listening corner with a ready supply of tapes. Children can record their favourites and listen to poems recorded by others. Teachers or parents can create their own tapes of spoken poetry to share with children.

In preparing to share poetry with children it is a good idea to practise reading the poem or poems first. Try to add part of yourself to the reading, through emphasising key words or adding humour or passion to your favourite bits. It is even better if the children have the words or book to follow as they listen. Encourage your children to recite favourite poems to each other; ultimately the aim is to teach children to read poetry to themselves and to want to do so they must first have appreciated hearing poetry spoken to them. They must have savoured the sounds of poems, and enjoyed entering into other people's minds. The initial sharing of a poem could involve many kinds of speaking: for example, whispering, chanting, reading slowly or quickly, or reading with added sound effects. A good poem has its own musical voice and this voice is the musical instrument through which the poem is expressed. No wonder Carlyle defined poetry as 'musical thoughts'.

Children should not only listen to the music of poetry, they should speak poetry regularly. After your first reading of a poem children can be encouraged to 'read along' with you. This may simply mean asking them to repeat words in the poem that they remember. These will often be rhyming words. Learning to say poetry is as important as learning to hear it. Invite a child to say a word or line for you during the rereading. A different child's voice could be used for each line or the children could be encouraged to repeat parts of the poem in pairs or groups. The sequence used in presenting a poem to children might include:

- practising reading the poem to yourself (perhaps tape this for the child to hear later)
- showing children what the poem looks like (the words on a page)
- reading the poem to the children (repeating this if necessary)
- inviting children to read or say parts of the poem with you
- encouraging them to say the poem in pairs, or as a group.

Children can be invited to call out the rhyming words of simple poems, for example the rhymes in the following limerick:

> There was a young man from Dunoon,
> Who always ate soup with a . . .
> He said, 'As I eat
> Neither fish, fowl or . . . ,
> I should finish my dinner quite . . .'

Young children often find little difficulty in supplying the rhymes 'spoon', 'meat', 'soon'. What does surprise children is that the original rhymes in this poem actually are 'fork', 'flesh' and 'quick'. This shows that you need not be restricted to given rhyme patterns, but can create interesting effects by supplying your own, possibly bizarre, rhyming words. In this way rhyming poetry can be an ideal means for developing children's phonic skills.

It is a shame, however, if children are limited to a diet of sing-song rhymes. They need to hear a rich repertoire of different kinds of poems, including those written in free verse. Poems need not simply be spoken, but can be enlivened by other expressive means, including hand movements and actions, the use of puppets, musical instruments and so on (for more on creative ways of performing poetry see 'Expressing' on p. 24). A question to ask yourself before you present a poem to children is 'How can I add interest to my reading?' It may be through use of voice or gesture that added colour is given to a spoken poem. Remember that for you as well as the children what is loved enough is not easily forgotten. A teacher described her own approach thus: 'I try my best to memorise the poem beforehand so I can give my children full attention while "reading" it to them. This adds to the drama of the situation both for them and me!' But if you don't love the poem, follow the advice of Ted Hughes[8], and don't try to learn it.

Reading

According to James, aged six, a poem 'is a kind of picture in words'. A poem consists of both sounds in the air as well as words pictured on a page. The shared reading of a poem which could take place during the Literacy Hour means getting children to both listen to the sound and see the words of the poem shaped on a page. The use of poems in 'big books' or copied on large sheets of paper or on overhead transparencies means groups of children can share the verbal and visual presence of a poem.

A poem is encoded in language. Helping children to crack the code and so to be able to read the words and so release the poem from the page is a challenging task. This means helping young children focus on the sounds of words (for more on phonics see Chapter 4), and also to think about what words mean. The importance of reading to young children has been emphasised in many studies, as has the value of learning nursery rhymes and performing other kinds of wordplay. Studies show that young children's sensitivity to rhyme is particularly important in predicting later success in reading. That is why singing and chanting rhymes can be so important in developing early literacy.

Reading aloud to children has a positive effect on developing early reading ability through helping children to differentiate and recognise different sounds (phonemes) in words, but so does getting children to see the words as you read to them. There is a problem in sharing normal-sized books with large groups of children, hence the use of 'big books' in teaching literacy in schools. Of course you do not need 'big books', nor coloured pictures, to teach literacy. Indeed many of the 'big books' used in schools today are of poor literary quality and the illustrations encourage teachers and children to rely too much on gaining meaning from simple picture images. A poem is a text made up of words: it does not involve pictures on the page but encourages pictures in the mind. It is better if possible to rely on text alone, since this forces the child to engage in decoding the words and not to rely on picture cues. It also encourages the creation of mental images. If you want a group of children to share the words of a poem then you can simply print them in bold on a large sheet of paper for all to see.

The following is a summary of the key principles involved in sharing the reading of poetry with young children:

- Choose poems to share which children enjoy.
- Present the poem with wholehearted enjoyment.
- Involve the children if possible in the reading e.g. by chanting some of the words.
- Repeat the reading for children to gain more from the poem.
- Follow up the reading with discussion and further activities involving the poem.

Young children find poetry easier to read if it is rhythmic, and rhymes help the text to be predictable. Nursery rhymes and the kinds of 'kids' verse' that are their modern equivalents, such as the Dr Seuss books, help develop phonemic awareness. The trouble is that if phonic or rhyming content is all a teacher is after then any piece of doggerel will do. As one child said of poems after listening to a nonsense rhyme: 'I like the way they sound but they don't mean anything.' Another young child said when his teacher was beginning a familiar rhyme, 'I know the tune of that' but the tune for that child had no meaning.

Children should be engaged in trying to understand the meaning of poems as well as enjoying the sounds they make, for after all, it is the meaning derived from a poem that gives it significance. Children should attempt to seek meaning from a wide variety of poems. Reading poetry with children can be a significant source of growth in vocabulary and comprehension if it is followed up by questioning and discussion. As Nikki, aged five, says: 'Sometimes you don't know what the words mean until you talk about it.'

Questioning

After reading the poem two or three times begin the discussion by asking some questions. Most young children do not know a poem is there to be questioned until they are shown how. The function of questions is to focus attention on the poem and engage the mind in trying to construct a message from the poem. If children are to read for meaning the general question they should be encouraged to answer is '*What does it mean?*'

This is best done as a follow-up to shared reading. The main purpose of this activity is to encourage children to think hard about what they have read or heard. This questioning of a text in a group is known by many names, adults engaged in this process might call it a Literary Circle, the Literacy Hour guidelines call it shared reading, other teachers refer to it as a Thinking Circle or community of enquiry (see p. 14). In this shared activity teachers question children about the text, so that they in turn will learn how to interrogate the text for themselves. This kind of interactive reading is what good readers do who do not simply read the words in their mind, but are actively engaged in taking meaning from the text. The questioning we do with children we hope later they will learn to do for themselves. But what kinds of question should be asked?

Children might be asked closed or open questions, or a combination of both. Closed questions are those which seek a single answer, for example: 'What is the title of the poem?' 'Does it rhyme?' 'Who wrote the poem?' Such questions probe knowledge about the poem and are either right or wrong. Open questions probe understanding of the poem and are open to a range of possible replies. The value of such questioning in a group is that children are exposed to a variety of viewpoints. They get to hear ideas they would never have thought of themselves. They learn that many interpretations and opinions are possible, and that differences of view are acceptable if supported by suitable reasons or evidence from the text. It is through open questions that children's minds are expanded.

Open questions that can be asked of any poem include:

- What is the poem about?
- Did you like the poem? Why, or why not?
- Can you pick out a bit you like and tell us why?
- Do you think this is a good poem? Why do, or don't, you think so?
- Is there anything in the poem you don't understand?

Better than questions asked by the teacher will be questions asked by the children themselves. This is because the aim is self-directed, not just teacher-directed, learning. Children are being taught not only about a particular poem but are also being shown how to question, discuss and evaluate poetry in general. They are being helped not just to understand a particular piece, but learning how to interrogate and make meaning from any text. To do this they need to be encouraged to think about, question, and comment on what has been read.

After reading the poem, and perhaps asking some relevant questions, invite the children to share any of their own thoughts or queries about it. One way of valuing their comments is to record them on a board, adding the name of the child to their question or statement to show you value their contribution. This list of children's comments and questions can form the agenda for later discussion.

What is clear from research into this way of working is that children who are used to asking questions, in a classroom that encourages questioning, will tend to ask more and better questions and come to think of reading as a process of active enquiry. Or, as Natalie aged seven put it. 'When you think about it there are always some questions to ask.'

The following is an example of a poem, together with some examples of closed and open questions that can be asked about the poem, as well as some queries posed by children[9].

Why?

Why is grass always green?
What holds up the sky?
Why is hair upon my head?
Why, oh why, oh why?

Why does rain go down, not up?
Why is salt in every sea?
Why is there a sun and moon?
Why is there only one me?

Why do bees buzz and birds sing?
Why do nails grow on my toes?
How long is a piece of string?
Why is it no-one knows?

Why is night so full of dreams?
Why do we have one nose, two eyes?

Why do questions never end?
Why are there so many whys?

Robert Fisher

Some closed questions about the poem
- What is the title of this poem?
- Why does the poem have that title?
- How many verses does the poem have?
- How many questions are there in the poem?
- Can you answer any of the questions in the poem?

Some open questions about this poem
- What is a question?
- Why do people ask questions?
- Who asks you questions? Can you remember a question you have been asked?
- Do you ask yourself questions? Can you remember a question you have asked yourself?
- Is it good to ask questions? Why, or why not?

Some questions about the poem from a group of six-year-olds
- What does 'why' mean? (William)
- Why does every line begin with 'why'? (Rosie)
- Why are there so many questions? (Nicola)
- Can't you find all the answers in books? (Paul)
- Doesn't a teacher know? (Sunil)

Discussing

When you hear a poem you don't always get it, but when you talk about it it helps.

(Katie, aged 7)

Usually the meaning of a poem is distilled in the fewest words. If children are to understand what Ted Hughes calls the 'spirit' of a poem they must integrate the meaning of the words with images and rhythms[10]. In this way they create their own mental model of what the poem describes and for this to happen they need to have some idea of the main point of the poem, and be sensitive to the relationships between the poem's living parts. Because a poem is so concise its meanings are often enigmatic. Inference and deduction are needed to make sense of what is suggested and forge links between what is said and what is implied. Even the simplest poems create ambiguities. Where exactly were Jack and Jill going? When did it take place? Why were they fetching a pail of water? How did they fall down? What happened then?

Discussion with others can help to deepen understanding through the sharing of ideas, creative insights and critical responses to the poem. This is not to spoil the mutual enjoyment of it, but to enrich that pleasure through a deeper understanding of what the poem means to the individual and to others who have read it. Many teachers find discussing poems with children some of their most rewarding teaching experiences. Young children are just at the beginning of the participative process. To get them to listen to the poem, share their ideas and pay attention to what others have to say is quite an achievement in itself. Sometimes a poem will spark off more interesting discussion with a group of children than the same poem would at other times. The advantage of the conventional Literacy Hour is that it can include time for shared reading of a poem. The disadvantage is that there may not be enough time for all the points and issues about the poem to be discussed. The trouble with teaching at pace, for a limited amount of time, is that it may suit the hare brains but not the tortoise minds. A creative teacher will not feel constrained by the clock, and will use his or her professional judgement in orchestrating classroom discussion and reading time. The oral groundwork of discussion, if it can be sustained, will enhance understanding and the quality of children's reading and writing.

Discussion can take place in the open forum of shared reading with the class, through group discussion or through discussion with individual children.

Organising group reading and discussion of a poem

1. Divide the class into groups of four or five who are able to work together.
2. A scribe is chosen or appointed (this may be an adult helper) to write out ideas discussed by the group.
3. Children are given a poem to read together, then silently by themselves, or they may hear it on a tape.
4. They pause to think about the poem (thinking time).
5. Each child is invited to say one thing, or ask one question about the poem, which the scribe writes down.
6. Children in the group discuss each comment/question which has been written down.
7. In the plenary session each group shares what they have written and discussed.

Topics for discussion with individuals or groups of children include finding words that rhyme, comparing and contrasting two poems (which do they prefer and why?), categorising poems (do they know/can they find another poem like this one?), ways to memorise a poem, sound patterns within a poem (alliteration), favourite rhymes, poems and poets and their own chosen titles for poems. Any poem can be discussed and analysed in terms of its form and its content. Here are some elements to discuss about any poem:

Form
- words (what does this word mean?)
- lines (what is your favourite line?)
- verses (favourite verse?)
- chorus (repeated words?)
- images (pictures in the mind?)
- metaphors (pictures in words?)
- sounds (sounds of words?)

Content
- story (what is the poem about?)
- feelings (is it a happy or sad poem?)
- thoughts (what does it make you think of?)
- title (what title would you give this poem?)

The poet Blake once said, 'What is most poetic is also most private.' What discussion seeks to do is to help children articulate their private thoughts and feelings and to benefit from what others, including the teacher, have to say. But discussing a poem is only one way of responding to it. There are other ways to express what we think and feel.

Expressing

> I like dance poems. (Kate, aged 6)

A child has many forms of intelligence through which to make a creative response to a poem[11]. Dance, drama, art, craft and music all provide ways to express and re-create aspects of poetry. Invite the children to perform a poem in their own way, illustrated with their own actions, pictures, drawings, models or musical accompaniment. Through any of the expressive arts children can enter the poet's world, and manifest the ideas and images of a poem.

The following are some ways of extending a child's experience of a poem through creative response:

Twenty creative ways to respond to a poem

- Illustrate a poem by drawing, painting or making a three-dimensional model.
- Tape record the group reading a poem and share this later.
- Get the children to close their eyes during a reading to 'see' the poem in their 'mind's eye'.
- Express the poem through movement and mime.
- Create a collage of words, quotations and/or pictures about a theme or poet.
- Make a mask or masks linked to the theme or poem.
- Write a letter to the poet with any questions you have about the poem.
- Visit a library to review, survey and choose poetry books.
- Invite guests to discuss and share their favourite poems and yours.
- Learn a chosen poem by heart and discuss the best ways of learning poetry.
- Create and discuss your own title for a given untitled poem.
- Predict the words missing in a copy of a poem which has some words deleted (cloze).
- Reconstruct the line or verse order of a poem which has had lines or verses jumbled.
- Put into poetic form a nursery rhyme that has been written as prose.
- Create music or sound effects to accompany a spoken poem.
- Listen to taped readings of a poem.
- Put some 'wrong' words in a poem and get the children to decide which and propose alternatives.
- Hunt special words or letters in a poem, underlining them in different colours.
- Ask children to choose 'my favourite line' from a poem, to share, display and discuss.
- Invite poets to share, discuss and answer questions about their poetry.

Composing

> Who alive can say,
> Thou art not a poet – mayest not tell thy dreams? (John Keats)[12]

What inspires someone to write poetry? Many poets would say that it is not nature nor the need to express their own feelings that most inspires them, but reading poetry. One of the problems for young children brought up solely on a diet of rhymes is that when it comes to writing poetry this narrow experience becomes an obstacle. It is little wonder that many children say they 'can't' write poetry and when they concentrate on making rhymes they often abandon the effort to make meaning. This is a pity, since poetry is an ideal medium for emergent writers.

In poetry writing, children need not be bound by the narrow rules which govern nursery rhymes, and are free from the grammatical constraints of prose. They need not write whole sentences with finite verbs, nor use capital letters and full stops, all of which emergent writers find difficult to remember even when they know the rules. In poetry, meaning can be expressed in the fewest words, provided they are the 'important' ones – nouns, adjectives, verbs and adverbs – and not the repetitive connecting words such as participles, which correct prose demands. For a young writer for whom forming every letter is an effort, poetry writing can provide an important freedom.

The easiest way into composing poetry with young children is through shared writing, where the teacher takes the children's words and ideas and shapes them into a shared piece. Much research points to the value of teachers modelling the writing process with their children (see p. 85), a process often called 'scribing' which includes not only writing children's ideas for them but talking through the process, discussing choice of words and phrases, cutting out unnecessary words, creating poetic effects and so on. Shared or guided writing gives beginning writers the support they need. What they do as a group, with the guiding help of a teacher, they will later be able to do on their own.

One teacher reports an example of this process in action with her class of 5–6-year-olds:

Autumn leaves: first poems with five-year-olds

We had read and discussed a poem about autumn leaves (in *First Poems for Thinking* by R. Fisher). We collected our own autumn leaves, and as the children described the leaves they had brought in, I wrote their words and phrases on the board. At first, their descriptions were fairly simple: red, yellow, round, pointed and so on. I pressed them to say what they were like and to make comparisons, and I got expressions such as 'thin as tissue paper', 'yellow as the sun' and 'crunchy as Rice Krispies'. I made a point of emphasising that this was their poem, using their words and ideas.

They went on to write a poem in pairs about their chosen leaf, with me focusing my help on one writer's group. We shared and displayed the children's writing in class, together with drawings of their leaves and read the 'class' and 'individual' poems in assembly that week. None of the poems was brilliant, but the children had begun to see themselves as writers (or 'real poets' as I called them). They had learned about the process of composing poetry, through jotting ideas, drafting, choosing best words, editing, proofreading and sharing with an audience. It was exciting to see five-year-olds acting as real writers, and to see the pride they took in their finished poems.

Here is one of the poems:

Autumn leaf

My autumn leaf
is red and brown
it has tiny specks
all over it
like a banana
it has a pointed end
like a star.
            Anna, aged 5

Reading, responding to and writing poems can enable children to voice thoughts and feelings that might otherwise remain trapped, inarticulate and unspoken. Poetry can empower children by offering them many voices, many messages and many tongues –

echoed in the words of Whitman[13]:

> Give me the song of a sound unsung,
> Give me the heart of a child that is young,
> Give me friends I can stretch among,
> Give me the words and give me the tongue.

Giving children the voice to express and share their experience can be one of the most rewarding aspects of teaching literacy. The following is an example of a five-year-old sharing thoughts about his special pet[14]. First he wrote it as prose, then he was shown how to write it in lines, as poetry, by choosing his best words and putting them in the best order:

> I have a pet koala
> he is all fluffy and grey
> and he is missing an eye
> when mummy put him
> in the washing machine
> he has only one black eye
> it is a pity
> he's stuffed
> 　　　　Tom, aged 5

Ted Hughes described the act of writing poetry as 'all outflowing exertion for a short concentrated period, in a particular direction'[15]. What the teacher does is to provide the direction, introduce children to interesting poems and support them in drafting their own. Once created, they can be communicated through publication to provide purpose and an audience, first in the writing group or class, then beyond the class in the school, local library or public space, or to a potentially limitless audience on the Internet.

Notes

1. Quoted in *The Poetry Book for Primary Schools*, edited by Anthony Wilson (1998, London: Poetry Society) p. 5.
2. The Kingman Report (DES 1988) argued that children's fascination with word games was an important foundation for the development of literacy.
3. One of the most influential research studies in this area was by L. Bradley and P. Bryant (1983) who found that children's sensitivity to rhyme was an important predictor of subsequent success in reading. U. Goswami and P. Bryant (1990) also found a link between the phonological skills developed by awareness of rhyme and alliteration and learning to read. For more on informal wordplay in early childhood see M. Whitehead (1995) 'Nonsense, Rhyme and Word Play in Young Children', in R. Beard, *Rhyme, Reading and Writing*.
4. The Bullock Report (DES 1975, p. 136) argued that understanding and enjoyment of poetry are essential to one another, and this dual focus is reflected in the *National Literacy Strategy: Framework for Teaching* (DfEE 1998).
5. From *A Midsummer Night's Dream* by William Shakespeare, Act V, Scene 1.
6. Samuel Taylor Coleridge (1827), *Biographia Liberaria* defined prose and poetry as follows: 'Prose is derived from words in their best order; poetry is derived from the *best* words in the best order.
7. In the introduction to their classic anthology *The Poet's Tongue*, W. H. Auden and John Garrett said: 'Of the many definitions of poetry, the simplest is still the best: "memorable speech". That is to say, it must move our emotions, or excite our intellect, for only that which is moving or exciting is memorable.'

8. In his anthology *By Heart* (1998, London: Faber) Ted Hughes argues that learning by rote succeeds only in creating an aversion to poetry. The heart, he says, is an organ of memory and what is loved by the heart will be learnt.
9. This poem appears in *First Poems for Thinking* by R. Fisher (2000, Oxford: Nash Pollock), with further questions for use with children. Many issues discussed in this chapter also appear in the introductions to *Poems for Thinking* (fisher 1997) and *First Poems for Thinking* (Fisher 2000).
10. Ted Hughes (1967) *Poetry in the Making* (Faber).
11. For ways of developing the multiple intelligences of a young child see R. Fisher *Head Start: How to Develop Your Child's Mind* (1999, London: Souvenir Press).
12. 'Who alive can say,/Thou art not a poet – mayest not tell thy dreams?/Since every man whose soul is not a clod/Hath visions, and would speak, if he had loved/And been well nurtured in his mother tongue.' John Keats, 'The Fall of Hyperion', Canto 1.
13. From Walt Whitman's published 'Song of Myself' published in *Leaves of Grass*.
14. This poem is reprinted in *Pet Poems*, edited by R. Fisher (1989, London: Faber and Faber).
15. Ted Hughes (1967 op. cit.).

Further reading

Beard, R. (ed.) (1995) *Rhyme, Reading and Writing*. London: Hodder.

Goswami, U. and Bryant, P. (1990) *Phonological Skills and Learning to Read*. Hove, US: Lawrence Erlbaum Associates.

Carter, D. (1998) *Teaching Poetry in the Primary School*. London: David Fulton Publishers.

DfEE (1998) *The National Literacy Strategy: Framework for Teaching*. London: DfEE.

Fisher, R. (1997) *Poems for Thinking*. Oxford: Nash Pollock.

Fisher, R. (2000) *First Poems for Thinking*. Oxford: Nash Pollock.

Bradley, L. and Bryant, P. (1983) 'Categorising Sounds and Learning to read: a Causal Connection', Native **310**, 419–421.

Hughes, T. (1967) *Poetry in the Making*. London: Faber.

Merrick, B. and Balaam, J. (1990) *Exploring Poetry 5–8*. Sheffield: National Association for the Teaching of English (NATE) Publications.

Powling, C. and Styles, M. (eds) (1997) *A Guide to Poetry 0–13*. London: CLPE.

Wilson, A. (ed.) (1998) *The Poetry Book for Primary Schools*. London: Poetry Society.

Chapter 3
'Jolly good I said': using poetry with older children

Robert Catt

For tamed and shabby tigers,
And dancing dogs and bears,
And wretched, blind pit ponies,
And little hunted hares.

Ralph Hodgson, *The Bells of Heaven*

Few teachers require a rationale for the use of poetry in the classroom. Children, and especially younger children, generally enjoy reading, memorising, reciting, writing and listening to verse and often express an enviable and uninhibited delight in the play of rhyme and rhythm. Such enjoyment provides a firm basis for learning and is acknowledged as a 'key skill' within the Programme of Study for Reading at Key Stage 2 in the National Curriculum for English (DfEE 1999).

Poetry in the classroom provides some very specific learning opportunities within the Literacy Hour because it draws attention to language itself in these ways:

- Children become quickly aware of poetic form: the shape upon the page, the structure of verses and the auditory appeal of rhyme and rhythm.
- Ideas in poems are often compressed: they sometimes need to be teased out, can even be expressed ambiguously and can create meaning on many levels.

As teachers are aware, however, poetry can also seem to be difficult and often there is a reliance in the classroom upon verse which, in being immediately accessible, offers very few of those opportunities for rereading and subsequent reflection and discussion which, for many, are an essential appeal of an engagement with poetic language. Teachers need to be encouraged to make an incremental shift towards an increasing variety of more demanding verse in the classroom. In so doing there need be no loss of that essential enjoyment but, rather, a gain in literacy skills as indicated in the *National Literacy Strategy: Framework for Teaching*: 'When pupils read familiar and predictable texts, they can easily become over-reliant on their knowledge of context and grammar.' (DfEE 1998, p. 4)

The selected use of verse can extend this knowledge: 'As they learn ... basic decoding skills they should also be taught to check their reading for sense by reference to the grammar and meaning of the text.' (DfEE 1998, p. 4). In working with the demands of verse, children will need to tease out such meaning by giving attention to language features exemplified by meaning, verse form, syntax and diction: 'As pupils gain fluency the forms of teaching should shift to emphasise advanced reading and composition skills at text level.' (DfEE 1998, p. 5). Such skills demand an *interrogation* of the tex. This is often best achieved through dialogue – exploratory talk – often prompted and supported by teachers' questions. Advanced literacy skills will acknowledge difficulty as children begin to realise that poetry can easily yield more than a single and correct meaning and that response and enjoyment are sometimes limitless. Here, though, they will be in the elevated company of one of the most highly regarded poets and critics of the twentieth century. The poet T. S. Eliot wrote:

> difficulty may be caused by the reader having been told, or having suggested to himself that the poem is going to prove difficult . . . I know that some of the poetry to which I am most devoted is poetry which I did not understand at first reading; some is poetry which I am not sure I understand yet. (Eliot 1933)

Poetry, then, provides an opportunity to move pupils from a use of language which is everyday and familiar, towards an engagement with compressed ideas, connotation (the ways in which words and phrases resonate with associated meanings) and ambiguity. Engagement with verse at text level demands that children draw upon their wider knowledge and experience as they learn to tease out contextual clues and to ask appropriate questions. Such engagement will involve children in the four language modes of reading, writing, speaking and listening and will also depend upon what might be termed a 'social literacy' (the ability to 'read' the needs and views of others in the classroom) which makes a community of enquiry possible. There is no reason at all why such literacy activities should become divorced from that world of enjoyment, expression and feeling which those who use poetry in their teaching will already be familiar.

Animals in verse

> Hi my name is Cheryl I like really dishy boys. I like doing a lot of sport, table tennis, golf, gymlastics . . . I am quiet good at art. I think that cutting down the rain forest and killing whales should not be done. I don't like animal circus's because animal's should not be made to do trick's that they don't want to do. (Cheryl, aged 10)

Much of the poetry I have used with children in the Key Stage 2 classroom has been concerned in some way with animals, and more specifically, our relationship with animals. Why? Because it works. The extract from Cheryl's autobiography, above, has some rich potential for the Literacy Hour including work on apostrophes, homophones ('quite/quiet' might be called near-homophones) and neologisms – 'gymlastics' seems a delightfully appropriate inventive noun for what, to the creaking bones of this writer, appears to be a mystifyingly elastic sporting activity. The interest here, however, is in Cheryl's concern regarding the treatment of animals. Evidence of what, for many children, is a major preoccupation can be found in classroom displays, the media and the marketing strategies of those many companies creating consumer interest in the young through association with animals and the preservation of exotic environments. To frame this rationale more sharply, however, it can be argued that engagement with the 'meaning' of such selected poetry provides an introduction to the cultivation of feeling – a compassionate understanding and concern for others – which, surely, is a principal aim of a liberal education.

Tasks

A sequence of activities will now be described using incrementally more demanding poems. Although the poems are introduced to children as texts, that is as printed words on the page, the following activities encourage exploration and are presented here to suggest dynamic ways of working within the Literacy Hour.

Ice-breaking: the introductory name game

A class of Year 6 pupils sit on chairs in a large circle within a drama space created by moving tables to the side of the room. I give my name – Robert – and ask each child to do the same. I ask children to stand and I explain the rules for the name game. I will start by looking across the circle at a selected child – I choose Sunita. I will call out her name and walk towards her. As I do so, Sunita will look around the circle, will select a colleague – Jo – call her name and walk towards her. I will sit in Sunita's chair, Sunita will sit in Jo's chair as Jo goes on to select another member of the circle, and so on until all the children have swapped places and are sitting down. Before beginning I ask for a prediction of the time it will take for us all to change places. Richard suggests 15 minutes; Manisha offers 32 seconds; there are some other guesses within these two extremes. I ask if someone could time us and Hamid, who has something resembling a deep sea diver's chronometer strapped to his wrist, volunteers. Our first go at the name game is a little hesitant. Some children forget to call out the name of the friend towards whom they are walking; others need to be reminded to sit down when they have changed places. It takes us one minute and 40 seconds and Richard has to put up with a little gentle teasing.

I now ask each child to name the person sitting on their right and this, obviously, works easily although I have forgotten the name of the boy now sitting next to me. I suggest that it would help my memory to hear each name again but this time tagged with the name of a favourite animal beginning with the same letter as our forename. To provide thinking time, I use myself as an example: 'My name is Robert and I like rhinoceroses . . .'

The group is now asked to stand again and the name game is repeated with participants urged to improve our time. Hamid acts as starter and time-keeper and, after the final child is seated, is pleased to announce that we have reduced the time to one minute and eight seconds. By way of memory test I ask each child to name the person now on their right together with the name of the favourite animal. There has been a good deal of forgetting. I tell the class that some of the work we will be doing will involve the use of memory.

Sequencing

i) Height

The sequencing activity is a useful prelude to subsequent textual exploration; it is also a useful control strategy. Pupils are asked to arrange themselves around the circle in ascending height order, without any speaking: gesture only is allowed. Teachers and children can find some fun in this activity with fine judgements being made between children of the same height, allowances being made for shoes, hair styles and so forth.

ii) Birthdays

A more challenging sequencing activity is for pupils to arrange themselves according to their date of birth: the circle begins with the child born nearest to 1 January and ends with the one born nearest to 31 December. Again only gesture is allowed.

iii) Verse

For this activity the teacher needs to have prepared a series of cut-up lines (part or whole verses, see below) from complete poems. On this occasion, teaching a group of 25 pupils, I had prepared fragments of text for each child. On other occasions I have asked two or three children, equipped with complete poems, to act as helpers. Obviously, the choice of verse will depend upon both the teacher's judgement and the number of children participating. The activity can obviously be varied with pupils given either a whole verse or even a single and short line or title (see below) where difficulties are anticipated. Each seated child is now given a piece of paper upon which is a fragment from the selected texts. (Although these are, seemingly, distributed at random, the teacher will obviously use her judgement in distributing the slips of paper.) Children are asked not to show their piece of paper to others and are challenged to see if they are able to memorise the words they have received. To facilitate this they are asked to walk quietly around the room repeating the words to themselves. At this stage the teacher can intervene bearing a waste-bin. Is anyone confident enough to throw away their piece of paper?

After two or three minutes pupils are asked to stop and listen. They are now told that they are each a part of a poem and are asked to find the rest of their text. A version of the previous sequencing rule is employed here: children are only allowed to speak the words they have memorised. Slowly three groups will be formed each comprising one of the three poems and this process can be facilitated by the teachers and any pupil assistants.

The children are next asked – again, only using the words they have memorised – to sequence themselves in order. Particularly if played strictly to the rules, this is a demanding problem-solving activity in which children must listen to and pick up clues from each other. It is, however, an activity within which the teacher and pupil assistants, acting as directors and giving prompts and clues, can play a crucial role.

Chosen texts

Choose animal poems to display as a text. There is a wealth of animal verse available, for example in *Pet Poems* edited by R. Fisher. For the occasion described above I chose 'I'm a Parrot' by Grace Nichols, 'The Ballad of Red Fox' by Melvin Walker La Follette and 'I Saw a Jolly Hunter' by Charles Causley (for poems see pp. 32–4).

Choral speaking

Children are now given rehearsal time and are asked to work in the three groups to provide a dramatic presentation of their poem in which readings are enlivened and illustrated through movement, gesture and intonation:

- Following my directorial suggestions, members of the 'parrot' group use their bodies to form the bars of a cage for the enraged parrot, each bar turning out to speak a line – using shrill parroty voices – then turning back to enclose the bird. As the poem concludes, the 'bars' fall back to release the bird with a chorally spoken, 'Can't you understand!'
- The 'jolly hunter' group takes a narrative approach incorporating hunter/animal mimetic actions, including the collapse of the idiotic hunter and the escape of a gleeful hare.
- The 'red fox' group provides a sober contrast with a serious, mystical and prophetic tone in which gesture and sequenced chorus were used to warn the fox of its fate.

Reflective discussion

The structure of the Literacy Hour provides opportunities for reflective discussion in evaluating the performance. Repetition is a feature of each of the three selected poems and teacher-led discussion is likely to give attention to the cumulative effect subsequently created in performance.

The children with whom I have worked are quick to respond to the emphatic capitalised conclusion to 'I'm a Parrot':

I'm a Parrot
by Grace Nichols

I'm a parrot
I live in a cage
I'm nearly always
in a vex-up rage

I used to fly
all light and free
in the luscious
green forest canopy

I'm a parrot
I live in a cage
I'm nearly always
in a vex-up rage

I miss the wind
against my wing
I miss the nut
and the fruit picking

I'm a parrot
I live in a cage
I'm nearly always
in a vex-up rage

I squawk I talk
I curse I swear
I repeat the things
I shouldn't hear

I'm a parrot
I live in a cage
I'm nearly always
in a vex-up rage

So don't come near me
or put out your hand
because I'll pick you
if I can
   pickyou
   pickyou
   if I can
I want to be free

CAN'T YOU UNDERSTAND!

However, on first reading, the Caribbean dialect words – 'vex-up' for 'vexed' (angry) and the elided 'pickyou' for 'peck you' – tend to be missed. Do they make a difference to the effect of the piece? I think so. 'It makes him' observed one girl of the parrot group 'sound a bit of a character'. Again, less immediately obvious but deserving reflective attention, is the phonic contrast between the taut and factual 'I'm a parrot/I live in a cage' and the airy cadence of 'all light and free/in the luscious/green forest canopy'. Awareness of this contrast is an implicit feature of the performed reading but, in my experience, explicit awareness needs to be prompted.

'The Ballad of Red Fox' is altogether more mysterious and elusive:

The Ballad of Red Fox
by Melvin Walker La Follette

Yellow sun yellow
Sun yellow sun,
When, oh, when
Will red fox run?

When the hollow horn shall sound,
When the hunter lifts his gun
And liberates the wicked hound,
Then, oh, then shall red fox run.

Yellow sun yellow
Sun yellow sun,
Where, oh, where
Will red fox run?

Through meadows hot as sulphur,
Through forests cool as clay,
Through hedges crisp as morning
And grasses limp as day.

Yellow sky yellow
Sky yellow sky,
How, oh, how
Will red fox die?

With a bullet in his belly,
A dagger in his eye,
And blood upon his red red brush
Shall red fox die.

Who is speaking here? Why is the sky yellow? The 'hollow horn' and 'wicked hound' suggest a traditional hunt with which the 'gun', 'bullet' and 'dagger' seem to sit awkwardly. The strange central similes – 'grasses limp as day' – give the piece a surreal emphasis. 'Spooky', said one child. 'It's death speaking,' suggested another, 'and he doesn't want the fox to die because he keeps saying "oh" and we say that when we don't want something to happen like "oh, please don't do it!"' Not all reflective discussion, of course, proceeds as smoothly as this. In discussing the similes I asked one group (and I should have seen it coming) why they thought the 'hedges' were 'crisp as morning'. 'Well, I eat crisps in the morning,' volunteered one boy.

Attention is now given to Causley's 'I Saw a Jolly Hunter' poem:

I Saw a Jolly Hunter
by Charles Causley

I saw a jolly hunter
　With a jolly gun
Walking in the country
　In the jolly sun.

In the jolly meadow
　Sat a jolly hare.
Saw the jolly hunter.
　Took jolly care.

Hunter jolly eager –
　Sight of jolly prey

Forgot gun pointing
   Wrong jolly way.

Jolly hunter jolly head
   Over heels gone.
Jolly old safety-catch
   Not jolly on.

Bang went the jolly gun.
   Hunter jolly dead.
Jolly hare got clean away.
   'Jolly good' I said.

'Jolly' is redolent of a caricatured social dialect and, again, quickly prompts the evocation of character. It is also something of a euphemism and it is interesting to ask children to find synonyms. Suggestions included 'silly' and 'funny' but were quickly rejected by children because 'they don't work'. There seemed to be no substitute because 'it's hard to say what "jolly" means but you sort of know it anyway'. Certainly it's an adjective with which children enjoy playing. Impressive in Causley's poem is narrative economy. The over-excitement and clumsiness of the hunter are succinctly conveyed in a way which demands children's attention.

Brainstorm

The class is divided into five groups and each group is given a copy of the poem which all have seen 'performed'. Children are given a few moments to 'brainstorm' some ideas about the character of the hunter in the poem in relation to age, gender, occupation, name, personality. Interestingly, response to this task is varied. Children, generally, tend towards stereotypical colonial or military personae but some deliberately work against such obvious characterisation in more inventive ways. One group created an accident-prone cartoon character, another provided a more historical slant with a musket-bearing poacher hunting on the king's land.

Freeze-frame

Groups are then asked to prepare two snapshots or still images:

- a picture of the hunter at work, pursuing, trapping or shooting an animal
- a picture of the hunter at leisure, possibly boasting about an exploit.

The still image is a useful and, probably, very familiar dramatic device and it is worth reflecting for a moment upon its value in relation to problem-solving and extension activities. Particularly under pressure of time (and three to four minutes is generally sufficient) youngsters must work together for maximum involvement and with an awareness of their audience. When the still images are being presented, the teacher can encourage speculative questions from the audience: 'Daniel, you don't look very happy. Are you a dead or a live animal?'

Extension possibilities include:

- the idea that this is a video *freeze-frame* from which the teacher, or a selected member of the class (and this is an opportunity to give responsibility to a diffident or timorous pupil) can move backwards or forwards in slow motion to illustrate preceding and consequential action;
- the use of a narrator or explainer who, either in or out of role, describes the scene;

● the incorporation, in the second freeze-frame, of part or all of the hunter's boastful tall story.

I am consistently impressed by the inventive quality of children's work with still images (for more on these see Chapter 7). One group, with seemingly little prior discussion, moved fluently into a pose in which a pompous hunter, equipped with drink and cigar, sat with his feet upon a prostrate animal rug, frozen in the act of delivering a hunting story to a listener, his long-suffering wife perhaps, who drooped with bored tiredness, watched by antlered animal trophies on the wall.

Moving on to more difficult poems

Children are each given a copy of 'The Gallows' by Edward Thomas:

The Gallows
by Edward Thomas

There was a weasel lived in the sun
With all his family,
Till a keeper shot him with his gun
And hung him up on a tree,
Where he swings in the wind and rain,
In the sun and in the snow,
Without pleasure, without pain,
On the dead oak tree bough.

There was a crow who was no sleeper,
But a thief and a murderer
Till a very late hour; and this keeper
Made him one of the things that were,
To hang and flap in rain and wind,
In the sun and in the snow.
There are no more sins to be sinned
On the dead oak tree bough.

There was a magpie, too,
Had a long tongue and a long tail;
He could both talk and do –
But what did that avail?
He, too, flaps in the wind and rain
Alongside weasel and crow,
Without pleasure, without pain,
On the dead oak tree bough.

And many other beasts
And birds, skin, bone and feather,
Have been taken from their feasts
And hung up there together,
To swing and have endless leisure
In the sun and in the snow,
Without pain, without pleasure,
On the dead oak tree bough.

This is a considerably more difficult poem which makes some interrelated investigative demands with regard to rhythm, diction and meaning.

The reading of the poem in itself provides a challenge. Should the teacher undertake the first reading? An inevitable difficulty if children read the text is the end-stopping of

lines which tends to work against fluency, rhythm and understanding. This is a feature
of reading which needs discussion. Unwarranted end-stopping can render a poem like
'The Ballad of Red Fox' almost nonsensical. The auditory sense demands the repetition
of 'Yellow sun, yellow sun, yellow sun . . .' and not the syntatic confusion of 'Yellow
sun yellow (pause) Sun yellow sun'. In reading for meaning, children should be
directed away from end-stopping to pursue sense by reading to the punctuation. One
way to achieve this is to read around the circle, each pupil stopping at a punctuation
mark. This is a technique which keeps the participants alert as they await their cues
and learn to run lines on. There are also, of course, opportunities for reflective
commentary. What counts as a punctuation mark and what kind of weight or
intonation does it signal? Thomas's 'The Gallows' provides particularly worthwhile
material for such a reading. This is a text worth exploring in some detail in terms both
of content and form. The anachronistic appearance and pronunciation of 'bough' is
likely to cause some difficulty and comment. As one child astutely pointed out, the
similar spelling c-o-u-g-h is pronounced 'coff' and '. . . this should be said like
"boff" . . .' Another, aware of Thomas's strong rhyme scheme, pointed out that 'bough'
should rhyme with 'now' and not 'snow . . . which would make it "bo". (Again, this
invites a discussion of homophones.)

The animals' revenge

A lively extension activity to which teachers might be drawn where they have a
confident relationship with a responsive class is the use of a free reading. Members of
such a group were encouraged to think themselves into the situation of a twilight
gathering of forest animals moved to some collaborative discussion of the oppression
they were suffering at the hands of an intrusive game keeper. I find this works best
when I begin the reading in a conspiratorial whisper, encouraging children to join in
with words, phrases or whole lines echoing the concerns of the animals. Such a free
reading allows the verse to be spoken by various voices and from various points in the
reading circle. Some elements are voiced singly, others in chorus, others in shadow or
repetition. After two or three rehearsed readings, clear characters begin to emerge as
voices are raised in agreement or counterpoint. These disparate voices – assertive,
timorous, plaintive – raised in common grievance in the refrain 'on the dead oak tree
bough' and repeated at the end of each of the four stanzas, provide a device for an
ascendant tone of strident injustice. These animals, victims of the hunter's terror, are
now militant and angry.

Another still image

Children are asked to present another still image, this time depicting the animals'
revenge upon the hunter. Images depicted are likely to range from the predictable: the
hunter hoist with his own petard with his leg caught in savage trap, through the
surreal: hunter waking in terror to find the animals of his nightmare palpable and
revengeful at the foot of his bed, to the topical and inventive: hunter tried for his
crimes at the international court of animal rights, a badger as prosecutor and a black-
capped owl serving the death sentence.
   This is a useful and potentially powerful pre-writing activity.

A listening activity

Causley's 'I Saw a Jolly Hunter' is a deceptively simple and succinct piece of verse.
Hidden from us is the 'work' – the idea, planning, drafting and rewriting – behind a

sophisticated narrative. Causley has talked about his writing, much of which is written in and about his beloved West Country environment. With the aim of making something of the writing process visible, I have read a prose account, taken from an interview with Causley, to Year 6 children. It makes for a good listening activity.

My mother saw. . .

> I come from a little town in Cornwall called Launceston where I was born and have lived all my life. My mum and dad come from there too. My mum went to one particular little school called St Stephen's School. She used to tell me a story about that school that I've certainly never forgotten.
>
> The headmaster of the school was rather a fierce fellow called Mr Davis. He wore a beard and had a cane hanging on a nail at the side of his stand-up desk. One afternoon in summer, and this must have been 80 or 90 years ago, they were all working away at their long oak and iron desks, all those children. There suddenly came a great knock on the schoolroom door. That was the one that opened onto the playground. It was a door almost big enough for a church. It had big studs all over it and a big iron latch.
>
> Anyway, over went Mr Davis to open it, and to everybody's amazement, there in a big white-hot blaze of summer light, framed by the doorway, just like a picture, was a man. He had a coloured silk handkerchief tied round his head and a kind of flute or whistle-pipe stuck in his belt. On the ground beside him was a heavy lump of metal – 'A bit like a cannonball' my mum used to say – with a length of very strong chain attached to it. At the other end of the chain from the cannonball was, what do you think?

Here I pause, then repeat 'What do you think?' Children are quick to suggest answers but I am anxious to give the activity some structure and I ask them to work in small groups of three or four. First, I try to emphasise the importance of deduction. The answer to my question should be based upon the text which, although giving little definitive information, has some powerful clues: the flute, the chain, the location, the time of year, the period which is probably late Victorian. Discussion should, then, be based upon insight and evidence rather than mere hurried reaction: 'A monkey . . .' 'a skeleton . . .' 'a ghost' have been uninvited and excitedly shouted responses in the past. I also ask that the answer to my question should be presented as a still image to include the man with the flute, the amazed headteacher, Mr Davis, who has opened the school door, possibly a startled peeping child and, certainly, whatever is at the end of the chain. Having presented their images, children are asked to provide underpinning justification.

A dancing bear

As with the poetry, the text allows for multiple answers. Here is what Causley's mother saw:

> A huge, ragged, dusty bear. A performing bear. 'Bruin', my mother used to call him.
>
> The children fairly gasped with surprise, I can tell you. I think the headmaster did too, but I don't suppose he showed it. Anyway, the keeper asked if the children would like to see the bear do his tricks. So out they all trooped into the playground. At a safe distance they all lined up for the performance, and the keeper began to play his whistle-pipe.
>
> 'Oh,' my mother used to say, 'that bear was a splendid creature.' It had thick fur and strong teeth and claws and great massive limbs and it did everything the keeper told it to do perfectly. It rolled and it tumbled and it marched on its hind legs up and down like one of the red-coated soldiers of those days. And it lay down and pretended to have died in battle for the Queen. It even did a kind of little dance or jig when the keeper played a particularly merry and lively tune. There was no doubt about it, the children enjoyed the show.

Yet, you know, as Mother used to tell me this story . . . I could tell that the effect on her and all the other children was rather different from the one the keeper had intended. You see, there was something about that bear . . . that huge, rather shabby, powerful, frightened creature, hot and filthy with dust, its feet torn by tramping the rough roads, its spirit half-broken. You see, that bear was so far, so very far from where it might have been, living naturally, wandering about in great cold northern forests, and free. And I thought to myself, 'One day, you know, I really ought to write a poem about that,' and so I did. And I called it 'My Mother Saw a Dancing Bear'.

What Causley's mother saw was, indubitably, a dancing bear. Rather than dismissing alternative answers as 'wrong', teachers are more likely to examine them for plausibility. The period, location and appearance of the visitor suggest to many children the idea of a pirate, seaman or escaped convict.

Children are now given a copy of Causley's ballad 'My Mother Saw a Dancing Bear':

My Mother Saw a Dancing Bear
by Charles Causley

My mother saw a dancing bear
By the schoolyard, a day in June.
The keeper stood with chain and bar
And whistle-pipe, and played a tune.

And bruin lifted up its head
And lifted up its dusty feet,
And all the children laughed to see
It caper in the summer heat.

They watched as for the Queen it died.
They watched it march. They watched it halt.
They heard the keeper as he cried,
'Now, roly-poly! Somersault!'

And then, my mother said, there came
The keeper with a begging-cup,
The bear with burning coat of fur,
Shaming the laughter to a stop.

They paid a penny for the dance,
But what they saw was not the show;
Only, in bruin's aching eyes,
Far-distant forests, and the snow.

'. . . *bruin's aching eyes*'.

Evident in Causley's poem is the effect of the compression of an elaborated prose description – the maltreated bear, far from its native land and climate – into a powerful poetic image: the children *read* the source of the creature's misery in its eyes. Within the framework of the Literacy Hour there are a number of complementary strands which can be investigated:

● stylistic analysis: the ways in which the poet's use of language works to particular effect, e.g. the immediacy of the keeper's voice conveyed through direct speech; the sense of gawping audience conveyed by the repeated verbs: they *watched*, they *heard*, they *paid*, they *saw*;
● comparisons with the prose piece, itself a written version of Causley's oral account, e.g. what has been omitted, what has been developed?
● the ballad form which not only facilitates reading but has such narrative appeal.

As has been shown, readers bring knowledge to the text and such knowledge can be both consolidated and developed by the teacher's contributions and questions. Embedded within Causley's piece is a succinct historical snapshot of what, at the end of the nineteenth century, would have been a feature of provincial entertainment. But such a historical account has strong topical resonance. Most of the children to whom I introduced the poem had seen television programmes about the maltreatment of bears, dragged from the mountains to entertain tourists in city squares in Greece and Turkey. Many were keen to provide accounts of similar scenes they had observed when visiting other countries. A complementary feature here is the education of the affective sensibility which, as I have indicated here, allows for the shared expression of compassion.

These classroom activities can, of course, be adapted and extended. Good textual materials combined with carefully planned activities can provide for a form of learning within what this book refers to as a 'community of enquiry'. Such learning is powerful because it is genuine, as it both builds upon and develops pupils' experience and knowledge. Such learning is also powerful because it is both interactive and what Bruner (1996 pp. 161–2) calls 'intersubjective':

> It is principally through interacting with others that children find out what the culture is about and how it conceives of the world. Unlike any other species, human beings deliberately teach each other in settings outside the ones in which the knowledge being taught will be used . . . It is customary to say that this specialization rests upon the gift of language. But perhaps more to the point, it also rests upon our astonishingly well developed talent for intersubjectivity – the human ability to understand the minds of others, whether through language, gesture, or other means. It is not just words that make this possible, but our capacity to grasp the role of the settings in which words, acts and gestures occur. We are the intersubjective species par excellence. It is this that permits us to 'negotiate' meanings when words go astray.
>
> Our Western pedagogical tradition hardly does justice to the importance of intersubjectivity in transmitting culture . . . teaching is fitted into a mold in which a single, presumably omniscient teacher explicitly tells or shows presumably unknowing learners something they presumably know nothing about . . . I believe that one of the most important gifts that a cultural psychology can give to education is a reformulation of this impoverished conception. For only a very small part of educating takes place on such a one-way street – and it is probably one of the least successful parts.

I have tried in this chapter to show ways of approaching the teaching of literacy that can develop such intersubjectivity and which, in a period of increasingly top-down curriculum prescription respond to Bruner's significant, timely challenge.

Further reading

Barrs, M. and Rosen, M. (1997) *A Year with Poetry*. London: Centre for Language in Primary Education.

Brownjohn, S. (1995) *To Rhyme or Not to Rhyme?* London: Hodder & Stoughton.

Bruner, J. (1996) 'Culture, mind and education', in Moon, B. and Murphy, P. (eds) *Curriculum in Context*. London: Paul Chapman Publishing/The Open University.

Carter D. (1998) *Teaching Poetry in the Primary School*. London: David Fulton Publishers.

DfEE (1998) *National Litercy Strategy: Framwork for Teaching*. London: HMSO.

DfEE (1999) *English in the National Curriculum*. London: HMSO.

Eliot, T. S. (1933) *The Use of Poetry and the Use of Criticism*. London: Faber.

Rosen, M. (1989) *Did I Hear You Write?* London: André Deutsch.

Wilson, A. (ed.) (1998) *The Poetry Book for Primary Schools*. London: The Poetry Society.

Chapter 4

'Playing with words': word level work including phonics, vocabulary and spelling

Mary Williams

Andrew, a Year 1 child, was reading a passage from an information book about cowboys with interest and confidence. However, there was one word that he read consistently wrongly. Each time he met the word 'cattle' he read it as 'kettle', showing that what he read did not always make sense. Most worryingly he did not seem to think that it mattered.

Why could Andrew not decode the word 'cattle'? One reason could be that he was relying on his sight recognition of words, and confusing two visually similar words that he already knew as part of his visual vocabulary: 'cattle' and 'kettle'. He might have been looking at the endings '-ettle' and '-attle', perceiving these incorrectly as the same. Or he may have been concentrating on the initial phonemes – 'k' and 'c' – knowing that these make the same sound in certain words, but choosing the wrong word. The syntax is unlikely to help as the two words are interchangeable, both being nouns. Reading involves a complicated range of decoding strategies, including sight, sound and context. What Andrew did not seem to be doing was using the context of the passage in order to help him confirm or confound his choice of word. So how could he be helped to read words correctly and with understanding?

The answer lies in helping him to use *all* the key skills of reading: phonic (sound), graphic and word recognition (sight), syntax (grammatical knowledge), and semantic (contextual understanding) in harmony. This presents a considerable challenge to the developing reader. We therefore need to be aware of the underlying principles which govern this complex process. Although these are not yet fully understood we do know what seems to work in helping children like Andrew to make progress and solve his problems in reading. This chapter outlines some suggestions for teaching the reading of words in an interesting and problem-solving way – that is, 'word level work' in the Literacy Hour – through the teaching of phonics, vocabulary and spelling.

Why teach phonics?

Research in both America and the United Kingdom has shown that is essential for children to acquire phonic knowledge when learning to read and that 'awareness that spoken language is composed of phonemes is an extremely important predictor of success in learning to read'[1].

Children learn to recognise and read certain words simply through meeting them over and over again in their own personal environment: for example, their own names, 'mummy' and 'daddy', labels on packaging, familiar café signs such as McDonalds or the names of television characters like the Teletubbies. This ability is linked to their memory and accounts for their instant recall of familiar words. The process which enables children to recognise words they have seen in printed form as complete units and to retrieve them from memory is called the the 'lexical route' to whole word recognition[2]. This accounts for the success of visual teaching strategies such as 'look-and-say' approaches using flashcards, the *Breakthrough to Literacy* materials[3] and other strategies for learning 'high frequency' words as advocated in the National Literacy Strategy (DfEE 1998).

Word recognition skills alone will not, however, be enough to enable children to process all the new words they will meet in their reading. As they become more fluent and read a wider range of texts the number of new words encountered soon outstrips the ability to remember them on sight. In addition to sight knowledge young readers need knowledge of the sounds that make up spoken words, in particular phonemes (the smallest units of sound in words) to help them decode unknown words. Phonic knowledge is essential for processing unknown printed words and its lack causes many of the problems encountered by pupils who experience difficulty in reading at Key Stage 2.

In the past many teachers have been sceptical about the effectiveness of phonics taught in isolation from the books children were reading, or when taught using unchallenging work sheets, or when taught without recognition that successful readers need to orchestrate a full range of strategies in order to become fluent in reading[4]. The 'combined model' in Figure 4.1 reflects the 'Searchlights' model of the National Literacy Strategy, which suggests that teaching should each time be focused on one or more of the key skills. In the combined model each strategy is seen as interdependent, each contributing to overall understanding at text level gained through the ability to read words in sentences[5].

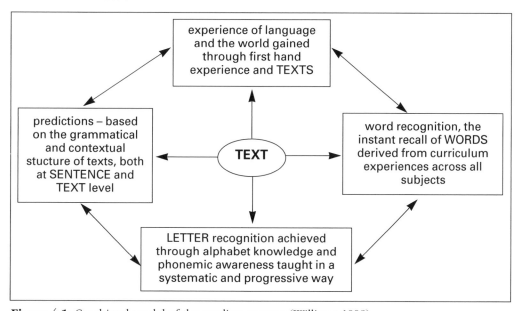

Figure 4.1: Combined model of the reading process (Williams 1998)

The effective use of direct teaching, as envisaged within 'shared' and focus group aspects of the Literacy Hour, offers one way that reading strategies and skills can be taught in an integrated and systematic way. However, individual reading encounters between pupil and teacher can also play an important role in motivating as well as assessing progress[6]. As Kate, aged six, said: 'Sometimes I like to talk to someone about what I've read.'

How should phonemic awareness be taught?

Phonic knowledge is important for unlocking literacy but how should it be taught? We first need to identify what children should know in terms of phonic knowledge. Taking the words 'sat' and 'flower' as examples, pupils need to learn that these words are composed of phonemes which comprise the onset (initial phoneme) and rime (end phoneme) and syllable sounds, as follows:

Word	Phoneme(s)	Onset/Rime	Syllables
sat	s-a-t	s-at	sat
flower	fl-ow-e-r	fl-ower	fl-ow-er

In developing 'phonemic awareness' emphasis should be placed on children hearing the phonemes in words. Children between the ages of two and four enjoy inventing rhymes, as is evidenced by their pre-sleep talking, when they sing to themselves and by the way they pick up 'jingles' from television advertisements or the meaningless, repetitive sounds made by TV cartoon characters. There is evidence that 'rhyming ability is present in pre-school children, and that children can solve rhyme detection tasks by at least 4 years of age'[7].

For instance, four-year-olds are able to *hear* and identify which is the odd word out from 'pin; bun; gun'[8]: this is essential if they are to recognise these phonemes in their printed form (graphemes) at a later stage. It is important therefore to give young children experience of rhyme and alliteration, through songs and poems in nursery and reception classes, to help them recognise both onset and rime phonemes.

Ideas for teaching initial phonemes/onsets

Phonic games based on multi-sensory approaches include:

- I Spy – 'I spy with my little eye something beginning/ending with . . .'
- Hunt the Thimble – hunt objects which begin with a particular sound.
- Twenty Questions: for example, 'I'm thinking of something which begins with "t". Can you guess what it is?'

Once children are conversant with the game they can choose onsets themselves but with adult support to make sure they are correct, e.g. 'Everything in my basket begins with "buh"; everything in my sock starts with "suh"'. As an alternative: 'Which is the odd one out in my basket: "bag", "peg", "ball" . . . ?'

Children also need practise in making analogies from one word to another, through being able to suggest similar onsets and rimes in other words. A survey in 1975 showed that the 500 most frequently-used words in primary reading books were reliant on 37 rimes[9]. Although the range of interesting and attractive books available for use in the classroom has increased significantly, replacing the often dull 'key word' series of the 1970s, the focus on a repetitive vocabulary in the early stages of learning to read has rightly been retained. Hence, attention to rime can reduce significantly the amount of learning needed by encouraging the child to make analogies from a known word to an unknown one, for example, from *light* to *right.*

Ideas for teaching rimes
(based on multi-sensory approaches)

- I Spy something which rhymes with -at; -en; -igh etc.
- Changing nursery rhymes and poems – Little Bo-Peep has lost her car
- Feely bag game: all the objects in a bag rhyme with, for example, ox. Children guess by feeling objects.
- Odd one out: all the objects on a tray end with a particular rime – except for one.
- Snap – spotting the same rime on a set of cards in picture or word form.
- Suggesting and collecting rhyming, humorous phrases, for example, a c*at* in a h*at* ate a r*at.*
- Rhyming pairs : could be an oral or a written activity, for example, say 'top/hop'. What can children give for 'tap/–'?

To return to Andrew's problems with the word 'cattle', children's attention also needs to be drawn to the sounds in the middle of words – the medial phonemes. Frequently, children look no further than the beginning of the word and may give a cursory glance at the ending but completely overlook, or fail to appreciate, the importance of the middle. For instance, in the example cited, the all-important 'a' in the middle of 'cattle' has been read as the 'e' in 'kettle'. This is where an ability to segment the word into its phonemic parts is needed and attention to the middle part of the word is essential. In other words, pupils need to be able to work from the whole word to each of the parts[10].

Ideas for teaching medial phonemes

- Choose a medial sound, e.g. 'a' as in hat. What other real words can be made using this phoneme? Examples are: mat, sat, cat.
- Odd one out: either in picture or word form, or both, for example: hot; pot; hit; cot.
- Listening game: which of the following have the same phonemes in the middle? Give a starter word, for example, 'feet'. Then ask the children if 'l*ea*f'; h*ea*lth; 'br*ie*f'; 'h*ea*th'; 't*ee*th' conform. This could turn into the sort of investigation suggested for Key Stage 2 pupils in the National Literacy Strategy (see below).
- What if? For example, what happens if the medial phoneme of 'dog' is changed to an 'i'? What new word is made?
- Looking for words within words: t*offe*e, c*offe*e, b*offin*. Also discuss strategies for dealing with this task: for example, going through the alphabet in order to see if real words can be made. This promotes metacognitive awareness.

Finally, as it is known that 'awareness of onsets and rimes precedes awareness of phonemes in the development of phonological skills'[11], it is important that a developmental approach to the introduction of phonemic/phonic knowledge is adopted, such as that suggested below.

Suggested progression for teaching phonemic awareness

- Using preschool games and rhyming activities based on *hearing* onset and rimes in words.

- Recognising initial phonemes in their written form and using these to spell words.
- Recognising rimes in their written form and using these to spell words.
- Recognising consonant digraphs (two consonants which make a phoneme) and blends – that is, two or three consonant phonemes said rapidly one after the other, represented by two or three graphemes (for example, 'bl' or 'str') which in some cases might also be a digraph (as in 'ch').
- Hearing the medial sounds in words.
- Recognising medial sounds including single vowels and vowel digraphs in their written form and using these to spell words.

In the National Literacy Strategy it is suggested that the learning sequence should be as follows:

1. initial consonants and short vowel sounds
2. final sounds in simple words
3. medial short vowel sounds.

It is vital that phonemic awareness be taught systematically, drawing on increasing familiarity with published texts and through the child's own writing. This is envisaged in the Literacy Hour, where the focus should be on 'decoding' during 'shared and guided reading' and 'encoding' during 'shared and guided writing'.

Extending phonemic awareness with older children

Children's phonic knowledge needs to be developed and extended at Key Stage 2 where they face the challenge of reading an ever-increasing number of new words in all subjects of the curriculum. Poor phonic knowledge combined with an over-reliance on word recognition can cause reading problems in older children. Research has shown that 'children who have good rhyming skills become better readers, and children who have reading difficulties tend to have a rhyming deficit'[12].

If older children need to extend and develop their understanding of phonics, how should it be taught? There is a current debate between those who advocate 'analytic' and 'synthetic' teaching methods, that is whether phonemic understanding develops alongside practise in reading through analysis of what is read, or whether it is something which should precede learning to read as advocated by those who propose 'synthetic' teaching methods[13]. The National Literacy Strategy advocates a mixture of methods, with the emphasis on synthetic teaching strategies for younger children and analytical learning strategies becoming important for older readers. We have found that older children often understand the need to analyse the sounds of words more readily than younger children. As Ravi, a struggling older reader explained: 'You have to think about what the different parts of a word sound like, then put them together to read the word. It's a bit like Lego.' Whatever the teaching approach, it is important that learning phonics is made motivating, as failure to achieve this can often be one of the reasons why some children, particularly boys, find learning to read unrewarding and boring.

The following are some ideas for teaching phonemic awareness with older children:

Onsets

- *invent alliterative noun phrases*, providing opportunities for work on adjectives. Examples are:
  names in the class or group, e.g. 'attractive Anne', 'energetic Edward'

disgusting food, e.g. 'putrid porridge', 'slimy spaghetti'

animals, e.g. 'bashful bears', 'coy crocodiles'

packaging, e.g. 'a jar of jam', 'a hunk of ham'

- *create alliterative sentences* providing opportunities for work on adjectives, adverbs the apostrophe, subject and predicate etc. An example is: 'Silly Sally suddenly spilled the soup on Susie's smart suit.'
- *adapt 'parlour games',* for example, 'The parson's cat is an adorable cat, bashful cat . . .', 'I Spy', 'Hunt the Thimble', finding objects beginning with a particular onset[14].

Rimes

- *rhyme to a theme,* for example, food is crunchy, munchy, chewy, slurpy
- *rhyming pairs* (including dictionary work)

  To be given to groups of children to work out from a given clue, for example:

  clue – obese feline = fat cat

  clue – ailing hen = sick chick

  Children then think up one each for themselves and challenge others to find the answer.
- *consequence limericks*

  Children need to be familiar with the genre, through shared reading, and the creation of a class limerick during shared writing. Use a familiar theme – such as those derived from fairy stories, for example:

When Goldilocks saw the three bears,

She ran as fast as she could down the stairs,

Thank goodness I'm free,

She shouted with glee,

But I'm sorry I broke all their chairs.

Once the children are familiar with the genre they could play a consequences game in which each child in a group writes a line and then passes it on to the next person who reads it and then adds another line.

Medial phonemes

Collect lists of words which conform to the same grapho-phonic medial patterns, e.g.: ta*i*l, ma*i*l, ra*i*l over the course of a week, drawing on a range of texts which are currently being read. Remove the middle phoneme of words; can children work out what the word might be, e.g. 'm—l', 'r—l'?

Children may find the more complex aspects of phonic knowledge difficult to grasp, for example, hearing consonant digraphs where two letters are represented by one phoneme, such as 'sh' in 'shoe'. The challenge for us is to extend their phonic and graphic knowledge, including more complex patterns and irregularities, through interesting and manageable activities. Through word investigations, children can explore the variety of ways in which phonemes are represented as graphemes in words.

Word level investigations

Pupils are asked to make collections of words which subscribe to the particular pattern, then analyse their collections in terms of the frequency of occurrence of each written form, e.g. the vowel/vowel consonant digraph (grapheme) for the 'ee' sound (phoneme) in words as in 'h*e*', 'm*ea*t', 'le*a*f', 'monk*ey*'.

Vocabulary

> Reading would be alright if it weren't for the words. (Gary, aged 8)

Preschool children begin to be aware of the printed word as they become interested in their print-rich environment, for example labels, posters, shop signs and street names. This is brought to their attention by the adults who care for them. In school, they should be provided with a print-rich learning environment through the medium of written notices, displays of writing and the giving of routine information in printed form, such as, 'Only four children can play in the home corner.' Children's vocabulary is gradually broadened through the teaching and learning of high-frequency words and through the reading of fiction and non-fiction books specifically chosen to challenge pupils' understanding and to increase their repertoire of words. They are encouraged to 'play with words' through a variety of games and activities including board games, audiotape games, use of computer software and phonic games. They should be asked to collect words which relate to a particular theme within the subject of English itself, for example by compiling a list of words which relate to 'TALK' – like 'whisper', 'shout', 'mutter' or 'bellow' or which refer to a cross-curricular topic such as 'foods from other countries', which might include such words as 'spaghetti', 'curry' or 'baguettes'.

As they get older children need to learn the technical terms that refer to the language of English itself as in Table: 4.1.

Phonic knowledge	Poetry	Writing	Linguistic language
onset	assonance	imagery	etymology
rime	blank verse	metaphor	morphology
digraph	calligram	simile	phonology
phoneme	cinquain	onomatopœia	graphology
syllable	clerihew	palindrome	accent
segmentation	couplet	parody	dialect

Table 4.1: Some examples of the technical vocabulary of English

Children enjoy learning about etymology, which is the study of the sources and development of words. This includes finding out about the impact of other cultures on the growth of English in the form of words derived from Greek, Latin and French, or, more recently, from the continents of Asia and America. Through this they acquire an understanding that language is dynamic. One only has to think of the changes to the derivation of the words 'chip' and 'gay' over the last 50 years to appreciate this fully. See if you can guess the meaning of the sixteenth and seventeenth century terms below:

- a lip clap
- a bed swerver
- gutfoundered
- pingle
- hippotomonstrosesquipedalian.

(Answers in order: a kiss; someone who is unfaithful to the marital bed; ravenously hungry; to pick at food; an extremely long word!)

An understanding of morphology is also integral to vocabulary extension work. A morpheme is the smallest unit of meaning in a word, for example 'car' is one morpheme; in 'housewife' there are two morphemes: 'house' and 'wife'. Of particular significance is the effect that prefixes and suffixes can have on the meaning of words: for example, adding the prefixes 'post' or 'pre' to the word 'date' makes them antonyms of one another. Analysing and investigating the structure of words can help children as they learn to spell.

Being able to do this is essential if targets for future learning are to be clearly set and fully understood by the pupils themselves[15].

Spelling

Spelling and handwriting are inextricably linked. They are a skill of the mind and hand. Even relatively competent spellers revert to pen and paper trials whenever they are unsure that a spelling is correct and may write several versions of a word to see which *looks* right, as 'spelling is best remembered from the finger tips'[16]. An example of this is shown in the following draft from a Year 4 child of a letter, written as part of a local studies project, in which he reveals several attempts to spell the word 'could' correctly:

> Dear Sir or Madam,
> We think you *cold* improve your buses by putting in a play room for little boys and girls and we think you should put in a TV. You *code* put a sofa bed in and you *code* have bed and breakfast. You *coude* have a computer and you *code* have a toilet and you *coud* put a guard dog on the bus becos evry one will want to jump on.
> Yours sinserly,
> Craig

Craig should be praised for his endeavour and for his final attempt of 'coud' which was nearly correct, then shown how to spell the word. He needs to *see* the word in its written form and then learn it in one of the ways suggested below. In addition, he should be persuaded to collect (as a possible homework activity) as many words as he can which have the same ending: for example, 'should', 'would', 'told'.

Children gradually develop a full understanding of a particular word as they experiment with it through trial and error. The ability to write, adopting the correct conventions of transcription, of which spelling is a part, emerges only over a period of time (see Chapter 6).

Stages through which spelling ability develops[17]

- pre-communicative – when any letters or letter-like shapes will do
- pre-phonetic – when a word is thought to consist of three letters e.g. 'prd' for 'purred'
- phonetic – when phonetically accurate, but not in the correct form, e.g. 'loveinglee'
- transitional – when there is a mixture of phonetic and the correct spellings in a passage of writing, or within a word
- correct – when spelling is mainly accurate but any pupil can revert to a previous stage when faced with new and complex vocabulary, e.g. 'queuemunication', written by a Year 6 child.

Spelling is linked to the visual memory and is made challenging by the many irregularities which occur in English; consequently, there is a need to learn the high frequency and medium frequency words as listed in the National Literacy Strategy.

Pupils should be taught how best to tackle problematic spellings, such as the following, which our research shows many adults find difficult[18]:

- sentence
- because
- February
- beautiful
- decisive
- independent
- separate
- dyslexia
- psychology
- accommodation

The question that any failed speller, whether child or adult, needs to ask is: 'How is it best to learn to spell a word?'

Ways to teach spelling

When teaching children to spell, aim to teach a few spellings at a time, perhaps three to four words which are connected in some way. Examples are: words having the same root – as in 'remind', 'reminisce' and 'reminiscent', or relating to a particular focus of work – such as the days of the week, or as part of the technical vocabulary of a particular subject – for example, in science, words relating to magnetism. New spellings should be taught on a 'little but often' basis with perhaps no more than ten minutes spent on the work every day. Similarly, we find that children are more successful if tested little and often (e.g. a small number each day), rather than by means of longer once a week tests. To lodge the spelling in the child's visual memory the well-known 'LOOK, COVER, THINK, WRITE, CHECK' routine should be adopted in combination with teaching children to use the following repertoire of strategies:

- Segment words into chunks and learn each syllable separately, for example, 'com-fort-able'.
- Look at the words within words, for example, 'straight/forward'.
- Teach words in the same 'family' (with the same pattern) established through a known spelling whenever possible, for example, -ea- words such as 'leaf', and 'each'.
- Offer children spelling rules, for example, 'i' before 'e' except after 'c' when the sound is 'ee', while reminding them that there are always exceptions to any rule.
- Whenever possible, teach spelling and handwriting together.

Children should be reassured that everyone makes spelling mistakes from time to time and that English has an irregular spelling system but that anyone can improve their spelling if they try. Encourage children to set their own targets in spelling and to take responsibility for their own learning. Children should be supported in developing their own strategies that help them to process unknown or difficult words. We need to motivate and challenge children, as well as provide opportunities for them to make discoveries for themselves. As Susie said of her own list of words she was trying to learn, 'I have a book of secret words I am learning to spell. It's great . . . it's my own book of spells!' Susie may not get all her words right, but she has learnt one of the most important lessons in developing literacy, that words matter.

Notes

1. M. Adams (1990, p. 123), as the result of extensive research carried out in America.
2. E. Funnell and M. Stewart (1995) who suggest that children need access to two routes for processing text when reading – a lexical route as well as a sub-lexical route.
3. The learning of whole words as relevant to the child, and as suggested by him or her, as in the *Breakthrough to Literacy* language experience approach of D. McKay (1970) which has recently been updated.
4. E. Ashworth in C. Harrison and M. Coles (1992) developed this useful analogy of seeing each strategy needed for successful reading as a section of an orchestra, sometimes playing solo, but frequently needing to be in harmony.
5. Unpublished PhD research (1998) by the author in which a combined model of the reading process derived from K. Stanovich (1980) and the Searchlight model (1998) was suggested as a way forward in terms of increasing understanding of the interrelated nature of strategy/key skill teaching in reading.
6. A timely reminder from P. Guppy and M. Hughes (1999) that individual reading encounters between pupil and teacher can be extremely profitable in terms of motivation and assessment.
7. U. Goswami in R. Beard (1995, p. 64) *RHYME: Reading and Writing.* (London: Hodder & Stoughton).
8. Research by L. Bradley and P. Bryant (1983) which led to a reassessment of young children's ability to hear the sounds in words.
9. U. Goswami in R. Beard (1995) op. cit.
10. H. Dombey (1998) derived from work undertaken by M. Moustafa in the United States.
11. U. Goswami in R. Beard (1995, p. 37) op. cit.
12. U. Goswami in R. Beard (1995, p. 76) op. cit.
13. Those advocating synthetic approaches are Sue Lloyd through 'Jolly Phonics', Diana McGuinness, Carmen McGuinness and Geoffrey McGuinness through 'Phono-Graphix' and, for older children, Alan Davies with 'THRASS'. Detractors include Henrietta Dombey of Brighton University (cited above) and David Wray of Warwick University.
14. See materials produced by Sue Palmer (1995) for the Longman Book Project.
15. QCA (1999) *Target Setting and Assessment in the National Literacy Strategy.* Sudbury: QCA Publications.
16. This quotation comes from Charles Cripps (1989). For further reading about the teaching of spelling refer to M. Peters (1985) and N. Mudd (1994).
17. Proposed by R. Gentry in 1982, drawing on G. Bissex's case study (1980) GNYS AT WRK, of her own child's emergent understanding of the spelling process, but as only one child was observed, some caution is needed in making claims on the basis of these findings.
18. From the writer's analysis of students' spelling errors in assignments over a ten year period from 1989–1999.

Further reading

Adams, M. (1990) *Beginning to Read.* London: Heinemann.
Beard, R. (1993) *Developing Reading 3–13*, 3rd edn. London: Hodder & Stoughton.
Beard, R. (1993) *Teaching Reading: Balancing Perspectives.* London: Hodder & Stoughton.
Beard, R. (1995) *RHYME: Reading and Writing.* London: Hodder & Stoughton.
Bradley, L. and Bryant, P. (1983) 'Categorising sounds and learning to read: a causal connection', *Nature* **310**, 419–421.
Cripps, C. (1989) 'The teaching of spellings', *Links* **24** (2).
Davies, A. (1996) *THRASS Primary Special Needs Pack.* London: Collins.
DfEE (1998) *The National Literacy Strategy: Framework for Teaching.* London: HMSO.
DfEE (1999) *English in the National Curriculum.* London: HMSO.

Dombey, H. *et al.* (1998) *Whole To Part Phonics.* London: CLPE.

Funnell, E. and Stuart, M. (1995) *Learning to Read: Psychology in the Classroom.* Oxford: Blackwell.

Gentry, R. (1982) 'An analysis of developmental spelling in GNYS AT WRK', *Reading Teacher* **36** (2).

Goswami, U. (1994) 'Phonological skills, analogies and reading development', *Reading* **28** (2).

Graham, J. and Kelly, A. (1997) *Reading Under Control.* London: David Fulton Publishers.

Guppy, P. and Hughes, M. (1999) *The Development of Independent Reading.* Milton Keynes: Open University Press.

Harrison, C. and Coles, M. (1992) *The Reading for Real Handbook.* London: Routledge.

Lloyd, S. (1992) *The Phonics Handbook.* Chigwell: Jolly Learning.

McGuinness, D. (1998) *Why Children Can't Read.* Harmondsworth: Penguin.

McKay, D. (ed.) (1970) *Breakthrough to Literacy.* Harlow: Longman.

Moustafa, M. (1998) *Beyond Traditional Phonics.* London: Heinemann.

Mudd, N. (1994) *Effective Spelling.* London: Hodder & Stoughton.

Palmer, S. (1995) *Playing with Language.* Truro: Language LIVE.

Peters, M . (1985) *Spelling Taught or Caught? A New Look.* London: Routledge.

QCA (1998) *Standards at Key Stage 2: English, Mathematics and Science: Report on the 1998 National Curriculum Assessments for 11 year olds.* Sudbury: QCA Publications.

QCA (1999) *Target Setting and Assessment in the National Literacy Strategy.* Sudbury: QCA Publications.

Riley, J. (1996) *The Teaching of Reading.* London: Paul Chapman Publishing.

Stannard, J., (1998) *An Update on the National Literacy Project,* Lecture (March 1998), Homerton College, Cambridge: United Kingdom Reading Association Conference.

Stanovich, K. (1980) 'Towards an interactive-compensatory model of individual differences in the development of reading', *Reading Research Quarterly* **1**, 32–71.

Williams, M. (1998) *A Study which Explores the Impact of the English National Curriculum (1990) on the Work of Teachers at Key Stage 2,* PhD Thesis (unpublished), Brunel University.

Chapter 5

'There's only one Michael Owen': teaching grammar and knowledge about language

Gerry Gregory and Francoise Allen

A Year 6 class and their teacher have just started reading a novel. Following a shared reading session the books are taken in. After school the teacher word processes the next page and copies the text twice. Then she goes through one copy, deleting all the nouns and leaving in their place gaps of uniform length. She prints ten copies – on blue paper. Then she makes further versions deleting the verbs and adjectives respectively. She runs off sufficient copies for a third of the class to have a verb-less (pink) text, and another third an adjective-less (green) one.

Next day, she gives out the copies: two tables get blue, two more get pink, and the last two tables get green. The tasks are to fill the gaps plausibly and work out the *kinds* of words that are missing. On no account must blues confer with pinks, and so on. The class is familiar with 'Cloze Procedure'; they have used it to consolidate learning in technology, science and history. They have also used it with poetry, attempting to supply what is *not* there by making maximum use of what *is*: e.g. rhyme patterns, line lengths, patterns of alliteration, and – above all – meaning. Accustomed to Cloze work, they are quickly on-task. They find the second task the harder: some of them can't find the term they need to refer to the missing words. 'Name', 'doing word' and 'describing thingy' are heard in groups' exchanges.

On the wall are five faces: ranging from very grumpy (1) at one end to very smiley (5) at the other. In almost daily use in this classroom, '1' tends to get used to record negative verdicts and '5' positive verdicts. By using the faces the teacher often gets pupils to vote, express opinions and hence collect *data* about their experiences and attitudes and preferences, rather than allowing the talkative and assertive and confident to appear to speak for all. She thinks of it as developing a sense of the importance of collecting *evidence* as against settling for a vague sense of how things stand – and as training for democratic citizenship. The question today is: 'How hard did you find it to understand your passage?' The children vote. As the votes come in it quickly becomes apparent that the blue (noun-less) group have found far more difficulty than the others. On the computer a block graph is produced to record the average scores relating to the three word classes. It is printed, enlarged (twice), coloured (blue, pink and green) and displayed.

We return to this classroom later.

There's an awful lot of 'grammar' in the Literacy Hour. . .

Year 5, Term 3: 'Pupils should be taught . . . to investigate clauses through identifying the main clause in a long sentence.'[1]

This is, arguably, the most 'difficult' item identified in the *National Literacy Strategy Framework for Teaching*, and one that, in our recent experience of 'delivering' INSET, many teachers find far from simple to grasp. It is potentially difficult for Year 5 pupils because in analysing a 'long sentence' one might need to ask if it is a *simple* (single clause) sentence – and long only because it has many *phrases*, or a *multiple* sentence. If it turns out to be the latter, then a further question arises: namely, is it a *compound* sentence (two or more clauses of equal status joined by a *connective* like 'and' or 'but' or 'then') or a *complex* sentence (a main clause with one or more *subordinate* or *dependent* clauses)?

Before pupils meet main clauses they should, for example, have been taught, as part of 'Grammatical Awareness', to 'match verbs to nouns/pronouns' (Year 2, Term 3), 'use the term "verb" appropriately' (Year 3, Term 1), and 'identify adverbs and understand their functions in sentences' (Year 4, Term 1). Around the same time as they set about identifying main clauses they will be learning how to 'understand and use the term *preposition*' (Year 5, Term 3).

. . . and there's a fair amount of 'grammar' in the 'National Curriculum', too'.[2]

At this point some readers might be wanting to ask: So what? Those of us working with English in the National Curriculum are used to the idea of teaching explicit 'grammar' knowledge. Albeit confusingly set out: for example, in that 'grammar' in the National Curriculum is sometimes used in relation to pupils learning *how* to apply the rules for making Standard English; sometimes it is used in relation to them learning *about* these rules and how to talk about them using standard terminology. (There's plenty of 'grammar' knowledge in the National Curriculum, too.) True enough. However, it is noteworthy that, in contrast with NLS requirements mentioned above, it is only in the Programme of Study for Key Stages 3 and 4 that 'clause and sentence structure' are specifically targeted.[3]

What 'grammar' refers to in this chapter

As we have already seen, the word 'grammar' means several different things – and this has been signalled by the single quotation marks surrounding the word up to this point. Sidney Greenbaum[4] identifies half a dozen meanings in an expert discussion. For present purposes just two points about meaning need to be made.

First, this chapter is concerned with 'grammar' in a *de*scriptive (rather than *pre*scriptive) sense. That is to say, we focus on grammar as *describing* aspects of how language works rather than as *prescribing* how language should be used.

Second, and amplifying 'aspects of how language works', the present focus is the study of how we make sentences. The emphasis is on taking sentences apart to see how they work, or, as one of our PGCE students recently put it, on finding out what's going on 'under the bonnet' of language. (In passing, it is often said that you do not need to know what goes on under the bonnet to drive competently, and *very* often said, for example, by students and teachers whose education has not included work of the kind this chapter explores, that you can be a highly competent language user without having *explicit* knowledge of grammar. Both assertions are self-evidently true. However, a case for teaching explicit grammar knowledge – that is, for helping pupils to make explicit a fraction of that vast amount of their implicit (grammar) knowledge which enables them, to paraphrase Chomsky, to generate and understand unique utterances – is made in the following section. Before we embark on that, it is perhaps worth noting that the analogy between effective driving, on the one hand, and using language, on the other, takes us only so far: the former entails a modest repertoire of skills plus the ability to 'read' and adapt to a range of road conditions and situations; the latter entails literally unlimited complexity and novelty of context.)

Is there a case for teaching explicit 'grammar' knowledge?

It should be made clear at the outset that we consider the primary business of the English curriculum to be the development of pupils as effective speakers, listeners, writers and readers. A plausible case for teaching grammar must show that knowledge of grammar, and skill in applying it, promotes that development.

The case against teaching 'grammar'

There have been many investigations into the usefulness and effectiveness of teaching grammar; and many studies have appeared to give it the 'thumbs down', for example:

> Wherever it has been seriously researched, the analytical study of grammar has failed to produce significant results in student writing across the board . . . It would be folly to ignore the avalanche of studies that point to minimal connection between the ability to parse, label, diagram, and correct exercises and a more generalized correctness, fluency and elegance in writing.[5]

> In view of the widespread agreement of research studies based upon many types of students and teachers, the conclusion can be stated in strong and unqualified terms: the teaching of formal grammar has a negligible or, because it usually displaces some instruction and practice in composition, even a harmful effect on improvement in writing.[6]

Although Tomlinson[7] has cast doubt on the methodology and findings of one such investigation, a study frequently quoted in Britain over recent decades to justify excluding grammar from the English curriculum, the trend is clear. However, what most of the studies referred to have in common is an appeal to direct improvement of pupils' writing as the yardstick for justifying grammar. In relation to this, QCA has argued that it may be

> time to try to shift the criterion by which the usefulness of grammar is judged. Walmsley (1984) has questioned the premise that the only justification for teaching grammar is direct improvement of pupils' writing . . . It may be more profitable to promote the teaching of grammar on different grounds: as a strand in the teaching and learning of language, which like all other aspects, compositional and technical, does not have a straight transfer into writing.[8]

We can find a plausible case if we look to grammar study for other benefits.

A case for teaching 'grammar'

There are two chief arguments for teaching grammar; both relate to the development of literacy.

First, it is useful to develop a grammar 'metalanguage' (a language tool for describing and discussing language). This can help pupils to describe, analyse, discuss and evaluate texts: their own and others. Arguably, describing a problem is a step on the road to solving it. Through shared grammar concepts, and vocabulary for labelling them, pupils and teachers are enabled to discuss, for example:

1. pupils' texts with precision and economy: for example 'too many adjectives' rather than 'too many describing words – you know, words like "red" – I mean, words that

describe names, er, persons, places . . . I don't mean the ones that describe doing words . . . or state words . . .';

or

2. the language of sports commentary: for example the use of noun phrases (see below) such as 'the England midfielder', 'the unorthodox Costa Rican', which offer a change from using players' names only or 'buy time' while they are brought to mind;

or

3. the use of 'nominalisation' (i.e. the turning of, for example, verbs into nouns/noun phrases, see below) in, say, letters from public utilities, as in 'Non-payment of bills may result in loss of supply' rather than 'If you do not pay up we shall cut off your supply';

or

4. the use of active or passive voice in newspaper headlines – and the resultant effect, and likely intentions, as in: 'Police shoot rioters', 'Rioters shot by police', 'Rioters shot'.

Examples 3 and 4 above suggest the development of concepts and related vocabulary that potentially help pupils understand and articulate how, for example, advertising and political discourses work, and work upon *them* (see also Chapter 10).

> There is much of demonstrable value for pupils in . . . learning not simply to look through language, to the content of a message but rather to *see through* language and be empowered better to understand and explain the ways in which messages are mediated or shaped, very often in the interests of preserving a particular viewpoint or of reinforcing existing ideologies.[9]

Regarding pupils learning a modern foreign language, and the special case of pupils for whom English is an additional language (EAL), a shared understanding of 'grammar', accompanied by a joint possession of a shared terminology, can sometimes allow teacher and pupil to refer with precision to aspects of English and how its features either mirror or differ from other languages in pupils' repertoires. Examples include: considering English in relation to some Asian languages, the positioning of subjects, verbs, adverbs and objects, the use or non-use of articles and modes of transforming statements into negatives and questions; and considering English in relation to French/Spanish/Portuguese/Italian etc., word order (e.g. positioning of nouns/adjectives and verbs/adverbs).

In the case of EAL pupils, our sense is that such explicit knowledge and reference are likely to help most those who are *beyond the earliest stages* of learning English, and when used in conjunction with 'deliberate exposure of the learner to an artificially large number of instances of some target structure in (English) on the assumption that the very high frequency of the structure . . . will attract the learner's attention to the relevant formal regularities'.[10]

Second, and related to the above, grammar study is valuable in helping to understand language itself: that is, it is a dominant means of understanding the world, of much of our thinking, of making (and undermining) relationships and of developing and expressing our sense of ourselves. The importance of such understanding is as self-evident as that of experiencing and understanding literature, though in our experience less readily admitted by teachers[11].

In addition to these fundamental justifications for teaching grammar, a number of others have been offered.

The following are examples from Hudson[12]:

- building linguistic self-respect: dispelling the myth that non-standard languages have no grammar;
- help in learning foreign languages;

from the Cox Committee[13]:

- some form of analysis (which may be more or less explicit) is necessarily a part of the interpretation of texts and of the production of accurate writing;

and, from QCA[14]:

- there is evidence that drawing explicit attention to the syntactic features of pupils' writing, in the context of an individual pupil's work and in relation to the type of task in hand, can increase pupils' awareness of how language works. This may in turn increase their sense of control over their writing.

Here, the evidence is neither produced nor referenced: given that which is cited above, the 'may' speaks volumes.

For a succinct rationale for grammar we believe it would be difficult to improve on the case made by the Cox Committee (above) for teaching knowledge about language: namely, to the end that pupils 'achieve a working knowledge of its structure and of the variety of ways in which meaning is made, so that they have a vocabulary for discussing it, so that they can use it with greater awareness, and because it is interesting'.

Teachers' commitment to and preparedness for grammar teaching

Successful grammar teaching depends on teachers' (a) commitment to it, based on conviction of its importance; and (b) competence, based on their own secure grammar knowledge.

Teacher commitment

The British press reported considerable teacher opposition to grammar teaching around the time when the government of the day introduced the first version of the National Curriculum (English). It is our impression, supported by noting the views expressed in INSET programmes and a small-scale enquiry which is reported below, that this opposition has diminished, though by no means disappeared. Furthermore, the National Association for the Teaching of English (NATE) has confirmed the importance of understanding grammar:

> The study of grammatical structures and systems allows pupils to explore for themselves an essential part of the rich complexity of language. It sheds additional light on the varieties and styles of spoken and written language, offering insights into how they work and how people choose to use them.[15]

A small-scale enquiry

During the academic year 1998/99 a questionnaire was distributed to an 'opportunity sample' totalling 35 teachers of KS1/KS2 pupils across a range of schools in the Brunel University/local schools partnership. Overwhelmingly, these teachers recognised the importance of pupils developing explicit grammar knowledge, as follows: eighty-six per cent agreed that, 'if pupils are able to analyse/describe features of their writing using grammatical terminology, this is helpful towards their evaluating what they write and understanding how to improve it'. Of that 86 per cent, 43 per cent agreed strongly.

The identical percentage agreed that such analytical/descriptive ability is helpful towards pupils' understanding, response to and evaluation of the texts they read. Twenty-nine per cent agreed strongly.

Ninety-one per cent considered developing such grammar knowledge important (given the other requirements of the National Curriculum), of whom 29 per cent considered it very important.

Eighty-nine per cent indicated their belief that 'the teaching and learning of explicit grammar knowledge' can be enjoyable for pupils; 34 per cent thought it might be 'very enjoyable'.

Teachers' comments regarding the cases for and against, and the priorities in respect of teaching grammar included:

on the 'for' side:
- We should focus on aspects of language children are having difficulty with at different stages . . . greater exposure (through reading) to more complex structures is partly the answer;
- Gives a shared vocabulary and helps with expression/fluency and pace;

and 'against':
- I would give this low priority. (Grammar) terminology is not child-friendly;
- More important things to teach – like writing process and developing lifelong readers and writers. Grammar not a priority for me. Was taught it very badly – in isolation, not related to anything 'real'. Was very turned off by it.

One teacher reported that 'Closer focus on grammar has led to improvement'. Tantalisingly, what sort of improvement is left unspecified. Another respondent reported: 'Year 6 top set cope well with grammar; average children in Year 6 find it hard.'

Teacher preparedness

Our routine 'audits' of the explicit grammar knowledge of both pre-qualified teachers and serving teachers joining our INSET programmes invariably suggest a gap to be bridged. Such findings confirm those of, for example, Williamson and Hardman[16]. It is clear that such a situation is hardly surprising, given the absence of grammar teaching from the English curriculum (and very often the modern foreign language curriculum as well) experienced by most serving teachers.

Hence, it is to our surprise that in our enquiry (conducted towards the end of a decade of a National Curriculum requiring grammar, and in the first year of a National

Aspects of grammar	Yes	No
wordclasses:	34	66
phrases:	49	51
clauses:	66	34
sentences:	34	66
active/passive voice:	43	57

Table 5.1: Percentage of teachers indicating interest in INSET on grammar

Literacy Strategy that has focused on it more sharply than hitherto) 74 per cent of teachers considered they had 'sufficient explicit knowledge of grammar to teach it confidently'.

When asked about the INSET they might need to develop their knowledge of particular areas of grammar, the (percentage) results are shown in Table 5.1.

Grammar teaching: the 'how'

> After they had begged me to reveal that afternoon's task, I reluctantly said: 'Grammar'. Groans slipped out . . . and skipping turned into slouching. I overheard Ben make a two pence bet with Ricky – that it would be well boring. (Pre-qualified teacher, 1999)

Let's start by returning to our Year 6 classroom, at the point where it had been found 'experimentally' that nouns were missed most:

With the *whole* passage (with deletions restored and underlined in the original colours) now displayed on the OHP, teacher and class are discussing the underlined words. The terms 'verb' and 'adjective' are recalled from earlier lessons – and the 'wordclass mobiles' that pupils made then, now turning slowly with the movement of air, are invoked. When they get to 'nouns' the word 'name' comes up and the teacher collects from pupils a list of the *kinds* of things that nouns name: people, places, things, animals, ideas. Someone wonders if, in a way, animals *are* 'things' – but is heavily, and in some cases indignantly, outvoted.

On slips of paper, the pupils now write their own sentences, with gaps where the nouns should be, and swap them with friends. (One pupil says it reminds her of when they tried to write descriptions of seashells *without using adjectives*, so that others could make accurate sketches from the descriptions.) Then the teacher asks them to listen carefully and put their hands up when they think they know the story she is about to 'tell', as follows: mother, son, poverty, cow, market, pedlar, beans . . .

The teacher now asks: 'Why is it so hard to understand a passage if you remove the nouns? And why was it possible to recognise a well-known story from a short list of nouns?' They think for a bit. Then someone says: 'Nouns are what it's about . . .'

In her grammar (and related) work, this teacher exploits opportunities that crop up while working on other things. Her grammar work tends towards the experimental, the investigative, the statistical[17], and she tends to work *inductively* (*from* language data *to* generalisation and naming concepts) rather than *deductively* (for example, *from* naming and defining a wordclass or phrase-type *to* consolidating such knowledge through working examples): '. . . we should start with shared concepts and experience and develop a metalanguage out of these, rather than deciding upon the metalanguage and handing it down . . . as a set of rules'[18].

When undertaking explicit study of 'sentences', for example, our teacher is inclined to start by inviting pupils (working in pairs) to calculate the average length of their own sentences in the writing they have produced in the last few weeks[19]. As pupils work on this activity, the teacher's attention may be taken by rising voices. She may note that some pairs are beginning to dispute figures:

> 'You reckon you've written six sentences on that page – but it's actually eight.'
> 'No it's not.'
> 'Yes it is. Number Two isn't one sentence – it's two.'
> 'How come?'
> 'Well that (pointing) should be a full stop – not a comma.'

Via a practical, statistical activity rather than by following a teacher definition (which anyway is likely to be inadequate)[20], these pupils are beginning to consider what a sentence is (and there are few knottier problems in descriptive linguistics)[21], to identify comma splices[22] (see below) and to focus on the need for appropriate sentence markers.

Contexts of grammar teaching

Arguably, grammar teaching is most effective when it occurs in the context of activities that are planned to develop pupils' competence in speaking/listening, writing/reading. Grammar teaching works best when contingent opportunities are seized, and when, if the work of enough pupils raises the same issue so as to constitute a 'critical mass'[23], a 'minilesson'[24] is 'delivered'. In summary, grammar learning is likely to be most meaningful and secure when it is incidental to and enhances other learning.

'Delivery' of a coherent grammar curriculum cannot, however, be achieved contingently: that is, *only* by exploiting serendipity and as 'spin-off'. A succession of structured grammar teaching episodes, albeit *expressly related* to other language and literacy work in progress, is essential.

A satisfactory grammar curriculum will feature activities of both sorts.

Grammar teaching in the context of other activities

> Knowledge acquired within the context of a meaningful writing activity . . . has a much better chance of being used and retained.[25]

Some examples of exploiting opportunities that arise may serve to convey the nature of such grammar work.

In the context of pupils' writing

- Study examples in pupils' writing of 'comma splices' (commas used where full-stops/periods or semi-colons are required)[26]; perhaps entailing use of such terms as 'clause', 'sentence' and 'sentence marker', and link this with study of published writers' practices.
- Find the incidence of sentence types in pupils' writing (simple, compound, complex; statement, question, command [imperative], exclamation), *study the effects* of writers' choice of sentence types, and draw on any insights achieved via improved redrafting
- Consider together ways of improving dull, imprecise pupil writing. Here, we want to caution against the widespread advice to pupils to insert more and better adjectives and adverbs. Regarding adjectives, there is much to be said for the George Orwell, Mark Twain ('As to the adjective: when in doubt, strike it out') and the Sir Ernest Gowers tendency[27] to think twice before using them at all. Arguably, writing is more often sharpened by precise use of *nouns* and *verbs* than by the addition of adjectives and adverbs[28]; and if effective communication is the goal, then to counsel pupils deliberately to import 'grand' words into their writing is likely to be the opposite of sound advice. However, with that said, in some contexts adjectives can be indispensable, as we saw pupils recalling in the lesson reported above. Invite pupils to judge the effect of adding adjectives to, or removing them from passages, or to repair sentences clogged with adjectives and to explain the improvement thereby achieved: such activities help bring these issues into focus by experiential means.

In the context of shared reading

- When reading an illustrated text, create Venn Diagrams to record the nouns seen *in the text*, those seen *in the illustrations* and those seen *in both*.
- Identify the connectives (and, but, therefore, nevertheless, although etc.) used in a passage, especially of non-fiction, explaining the work they do and attempting to define them.
- Pupils place their copies of a text face down with the teacher reading on, stopping after the first word of a sentence (e.g. 'Although . . .' or 'Moreover . . .') and asking pupils to predict the structure of the sentence in question.
- Examine the verbs/adjectives used in telling a story[29].
- Notice the use of verbs in the passive voice in fiction: for instance, in a passage of Chapter 5 of *Jane Eyre*:

    to this inferior class I was *called*, and *placed* at the bottom of it . . . the day's Collect *was repeated*, then certain texts of Scripture *were said* . . . By the time that exercise *was terminated*, day had fully dawned . . . the classes were *marshalled* and *marched* into another room for breakfast . . .'

Then discuss the impression of *lack of agency* on the part of Jane and her classmates at Lowood School: the effect of suggesting that they were mostly having things done *to* them.

In the context of Media Education work (see also Chapter 10)

Pupils study:
- sentence/paragraph lengths/structures within broadsheets and tabloids.
- reasons for/effects of widespread use of *phrases* in newspaper reports ('Attractive brunette Maria, London-born animal rights campaigner and mother of three . . .').
- the nature of headlines (Are they 'sentences'? What wordclasses predominate/ disappear? ('COACH SEAT BELTS SAFETY VICTORY'; 'GERBIL GETS GENES') What verbs/nouns are in especially common use (AXE/BID/ROW/SHOCK) and why? What verb *tense* is most used, and why? How are adjectivals formed to achieve compression? ('MASKED RAIDER BITTEN BY *HAVE-A-GO* GRANNY')[30]
- the incidence/effects of 'nominalisation'. This is the turning of verbs, especially, into nouns so that, among other things, human actions are turned into 'things', with often a loss of 'agency' and a hiding of responsibility. For example, the excuse note that refers to a 'family commitment' as opposed to saying 'We went to a party'; or the military briefing that refers to 'collateral damage' rather than saying 'We bombed a hospital by mistake'[31]. Nominalisation usually occurs more in written than in spoken language and tends to be valued by teachers where it occurs in pupil writing. For example: 'Many people are concerned that scientists are trying out new cosmetics on animals', may strike teachers (semi- or unconsciously) as linguistically less sophisticated than: 'There is widespread concern at animal testing of new cosmetics.'
    (This raises a number of issues about writing development and about the sorts of language teachers value, and why.)

Pupils might study the structural advantages of nominalisation, for instance, that a writer is able to load meaning into a clause by piling up nouns or noun phrases, whereas there will normally be just the one verb. Also that a 'technical' term can be substituted for a long-winded description of the same thing: for example, 'enjambement' instead of something like 'overflowing the meaning from a line of poetry into the one that follows it (i.e. following punctuation and sentence-structure) so that the verse-division is ignored in reading'.

In the context of work on advertising/commercial language uses

Pupils search through a pile of newspapers to find the adjectives most used in advertisements for domestic property or for holiday resorts and make graphs to represent the findings. They can then explore the possible purposes and evident effects of the choice of adjectives and create 'anti-ads', substituting unlikely adjectives and so forth. Through recourse to a journals collection in the local library it is possible to compare the adjectives pupils find with those used in advertisements 50 or 100 years before, hence raising the (non-grammar) issue of codes of law and practice governing advertising today. This will help establish that there are different *kinds* of adjectives, for instance, *spacious* rooms and *dining*-rooms[32]. Perhaps teacher and class will get so interested in adjectives that they look up the origins of the *word* 'adjective': they will pass from puzzlement at, to fascination with its relation to the word 'jet' (and the French 'jeter'); and from there note the significance, going far beyond grammar, of an early use recorded in the Oxford English Dictionary: 'The women were treated as adjective beings' (i.e. additional: appendages to the men) (Grote, 1794–1871).

'Set-piece' grammar lessons

> As far as my pupils are concerned, they shall not parse. (Teacher)[33]

Here we have in mind teaching lessons that are specified in schemes of work to ensure coherent coverage of appropriate grammar concepts: these are 'core' lessons to which the above activities are additional.

Many such lessons, for many teachers, will draw on published teaching materials. The latter are inevitably uneven; some may even contain information that is downright 'wrong'. A good deal of recently produced material consists of fairly standard grammar exercises published in a modern idiom: no change there, except in the modernist 'designer' packaging of traditional fare. Much material, perhaps inevitably, offers simplified, unproblematic language examples to which it is fairly straightforward to attach simple grammatical labels: '. . . the practise exercises in grammar books are carefully crafted to be relatively easy; they do not give students the opportunity to grasp the critical features of a concept like *sentence*'[34].

The work of Sue Palmer (e.g. in her articles and Longman Book Project) and of Jim Crinson[35] are valuable, partly because they draw on an extensive study of linguistics and are a rich source of 'set-piece' grammar lessons.

Some material written for teachers or other adults – includes activities that might arguably be adapted for use with pupils[36]. The two language encyclopaedias edited by David Crystal[37] provide raw material for a range of language, including grammar work.

In addition to using published grammar resources, teachers will find it useful to keep and draw on a file of other material that crops up: e.g. items such as the above from other language activities, environmental print, junk mail, journalism and spoken utterances transcribed[38].

Examples from the latter categories that cropped up while this was being drafted are:

1. 'Having worn the same dress to two consecutive balls, the Prince of Wales approached (Lillie Langtry) and exclaimed: "That damned dress again".'[39]
2. 'Having served their sentences, their houses are firebombed.'
3. 'Like an awful lot of rich men, his finances are complex.'

Pupils might explore why, although meaning is arguably clear in each case, the *actual construction* of these sentences *seems* to suggest that the Prince wore the dress; that houses served prison sentences; and that finances are like men. From there it might be a matter of finding grammatical terms, like 'unattached' or 'misrelated' or 'dangling' participles ('having' in (1) and (2) above, for example), to use in crystallising such analyses.

It is a truism that having to explain a joke kills it stone dead. However, teachers may consider it worthwhile inviting pupils, after enjoying such items as the following, to explain, using grammatical terms, the source of any humour that may strike them:

1. GENERAL FLIES BACK TO FRONT (World War II headline).
2. Girls like reading more than boys.
3. MPs discussed fox-hunting in the House of Commons.
4. We dispense with accuracy (sign in chemist's shop).
5. Please sign the form and return in the envelope provided.
6. This door is alarmed.
7. GIANT WAVES DOWN FUNNEL (much-quoted headline).
8. (a) My wife who is French has lived in England for ten years. . .
   (b) My wife, who is French, has lived in England for ten years. . .
9. Doctor: Did you drink your medicine after your bath, as I told you to?
   Patient: No. By the time I'd drunk the bath I couldn't manage the medicine.

Attempts at explanation of some of the above are given in an endnote[40].

There is a good deal of grammar 'mileage' in studying:

- recipes (nouns and the occasional adjective among the ingredients – why? verbs and the occasional adverb within the 'method' – why?)
- menus (adjectivals like 'farm-fresh', 'drizzled', 'topped with coffee cream', 'smothered with gooey fudge frosty'. . .)
- product names (e.g. most of a clause used as an adjective-noun in 'I Can't Believe it's not Butter'; the similar use of a subjunctive fragment – from Rudyard Kipling's poem 'Recessional' – in the name: 'The Richmond and Twickenham Lest-We-Forget Association').

These exemplify the remarkable flexibility of English, which allows words, phrases and clauses to do a variety of jobs in utterances. It is for this reason that care is needed in teaching pupils that, for example, a word is of a particular wordclass and still more in associating it with a particular colour[41].

Reference may be made to the pictures on the classroom wall. They may be full of nouns, to which adjectives can be attached, and verbs attracting appropriate adverbs, and whose description entails the use of prepositions: lady *beside* a spinet, cat *beneath* a table, table *by* the wall, seat *near* a cornfield.

Games have their place in grammar teaching, for example:

- Tie labels or stick 'Post-Its' on 'nouns' in the classroom.
- In drama, develop an adverbial dance (e.g. moving stealthily; confidently; cautiously; assertively; proudly . . .)
- Enact prepositions (*under* the desk, *in* the stock cupboard, *behind* the door) – or, more accurately, acting the prepositional phrases they introduce. (A pre-qualified teacher recently testified to the popularity of this: 'We played the preposition game. A few days later I noticed kids playing it during 'wet play'.)
- In reading a passage aloud substitute 'sausages' for every noun (some authorities prefer 'coffee-pot', 'flump' etc!)

- Pupils are asked to bring in copies of poems cut into chunks for other pupils to reassemble. Were any chunks 'full sentences'? Why do you think so? (A 'back door' into sentence study.)
- Pupils produce lists, as follows: town, river, country, boy's name, girl's name, fruit, vegetable, animal, each starting with the same letter (Liverpool, Loire, Luxembourg . . .) Why do some words have capitals? (This potentially consolidates understanding of proper nouns. For further work on proper nouns, *The Guinness Book of Names* is a rich, suggestive resource.)
- Make and use 'sentence-machines' (from kitchen-roll tubing, card and tape).
- Adapt a long-established playground activity (called 'fortune-tellers' in some playgrounds), making and using grammar 'quizzers'[42].

Such gaming activity shades off into more familiar grammar exercises, for example:

- Reverse *subject* and *object* for humorous effect (*Mandy* rode a *horse*).
- Identify that what wordclass a word belongs to depends on how it is used in a particular utterance (shop, bill, round, table, box).
- Finding (usually *noun*) phrases on the spines of books in the class library (*Charlotte's Web*, *The Iron Man*, *Harry Potter and the Philosopher's Stone*, *The Borrowers*) to consolidate understanding of the concept 'phrase'.
- Matching subjects and predicates:
  The League Champions   like to go shopping on Saturday morning
  Mandy and her Mum   did a lap of honour
  helps to reinforce these concepts. (Compare the teacher who started a lesson on the notion of the *subject* of a sentence by referring to our being The Queen's *subjects*. This established the expectation that a sentence subject will be human led to confusion when the class reached: 'An angry rhinoceros lumbered into view.')
- Identify (as in the above lesson) the wordclasses of missing words and fill gaps appropriately.
  (A variation on the former part of this is using nonsense verse like 'Jabberwocky' by Lewis Carroll. *Slithy* and *toves* are likely to be identified as adjective and noun, respectively. However, given that we can't look them up, how do we know this? The answer is, of course, that we draw on our understanding of sentence structure. This potentially reinforces understanding that which wordclass a word should be allocated to depends on the work it does: the slot it occupies in an utterance. See again the caution, above, regarding pigeon-holing particular words within particular wordclasses, and especially associating them with particular colours further to strengthen the identification.)
- Compose theme poems following set wordclass patterns, for example, each line to contain adjective, noun, verb and adverb, or lines to contain specified components:
  noun,
  adjective adjective,
  verb verb verb,
  noun noun noun noun etc.
- Write a few lines about a topic, each starting with one preposition and containing another.
- Write a scene from a play using all four sentence types.

A role for information and communication technology (ICT)

Use of ICT played a part in the lesson we visited earlier in this chapter and there is much 'grammar mileage' bound up with use of ICT generally (see also Chapter 9). For example: altering *sequences* of clauses/phrases within utterances so as to understand the changes of emphasis this can achieve; similarly, transforming sentences from active to passive (see above); combining clauses to form multiple sentences; highlighting all adverbs, say, and inviting pupils to identify what the highlighted words have in common and then attaching the agreed label ('adverb'); inviting pupils to make the changes to a well-known poem suggested by a grammar checker and to discuss the effects of such changes; in a passage of 'teen fiction' finding/replacing female with male names, and vice versa, and noting the effects: e.g. do the linked verbs, adverbs, adjectives etc. still feel appropriate, or are some strongly linked with males/females?

Conclusion

A child does not need any special cognitive abilities or teaching to be able to think and talk about language.'[13]

This chapter has suggested a modest role for grammar in the English curriculum, and has offered suggestions as to how grammar might be effectively and enjoyably taught. The challenge we have posed is that, discarding the unproductive aspects of the grammar curriculum of the 1950s and earlier, we help pupils develop their understanding of language in use, both their own and that of others, and of the options from which we all choose in our daily attempts to make meaning.

Time for a final visit to our Year 6 classroom . . .

There is still plenty more 'mileage' in the OHP passage. The teacher now asks for two lists: of nouns starting with lower-case and capital letters, respectively. This leads to discussion, definition and labelling of 'proper nouns'. The teacher makes a mental note that next time they work on the history of English she will bring in her copy of *Gulliver's Travels* to show them how *all* English nouns were once capitalised, as in German they still are. Still pondering proper nouns, someone sings, *sotto voce*, 'There's only one Michael Owen'; the teacher hears it and remarks that there are grammar lessons to be had everywhere, even on the football terraces!

Now two more lists: nouns referring to just one thing, and nouns where there are two or more. (The second list includes 'craftsmen' and 'gentlemen', but the majority end in 's', including 'experts' and 'ladies'.) The books are given out and the incidence of '-s' plurals and other types is researched. Another block graph results. One of the words found is 'donkeys', and someone asks why it becomes 'donkeys' while lady' becomes 'ladies'. There is talk of when there is and when there isn't a vowel before the '-y-'. The teacher considers mentioning where the different plural forms have come from, but decides, again, to save it for the aforementioned forthcoming lesson in her language change series. . .

Notes

1. Department for Education and Employment (DfEE) (1998) *The National Literacy Strategy: Framework for Teaching.* London: HMSO, p. 48.
2. DFEE (1999) *English in the National Curriculum.* London: HMSO.
3. DFEE (1999) *English in the National Curriculum.* London: HMSO.
4. S. Greenbaum, (1988) *Good English and the Grammarian* (Ch.2). Harlow: Longman.
5. S. D'Eloia (1977) 'The uses – and limits – of grammar', *Journal of Basic Writing* **1**, Spring/Summer, 1–20.
6. R. Braddock *et al.* (1963) *Research in Written Composition.* Urbana, Ill.: National Council of Teachers of English, cited in P. Hartwell, 'Grammar, grammars, and the teaching of grammar', *College English* **47** (2), February 1985, 105. In this country, Connie and Harold Rosen wrote

(in *The Language of Primary School Children*, London: Penguin, 1973, p. 253): 'We have assumed that the teaching of grammar in the primary school is as discredited as teaching capes and bays and copperplate . . . What teachers have discovered for themselves is that . . . the return for trying to teach children about language was very low *in terms of its effect on how they used language* . . . Clearly, "the more you know about the language the better you use it" does not stand up to examination.' (Emphasis added.)

7. D.Tomlinson (1994) 'Errors in the research into the effectiveness of grammar teaching', *English in Education* **28**(1), Spring, 20–6.

8. Quality and Curriculum Authority (QCA) (1998) *The Grammar Papers*. London: QCA, p. 55. Details of the article alluded to are: J. Walmsley, 'The uselessness of formal grammar?' *Committee for Linguistics in Education Working Paper No.2* Birmingham: Language Studies Unit, Aston University (1984 – reprinted 1993).

9. R. Carter (1990) *Knowledge about Language and the Curriculum*. London: Hodder & Stoughton, p. 108. Note also the 'cultural analysis' role of the subject English: DES (1989) *English for Ages 5 to 16*. London: HMSO, para. 2.24.

10. T. D. Terrell (1991) 'The role of grammar instruction in a communicative approach', *The Modern Language Journal* **75**(i), p. 59.

11. Quality and Curriculum Authority (QCA) (1998) *The Grammar Papers*. London: QCA, p. 55.

12. R. Hudson (1992) *Teaching Grammar: a Guide for the National Curriculum*. Oxford: Blackwell, pp. 181–8.

13. Department of Education and Science (DES) (1989) *English for Ages 5 to 16*. London: HMSO.

14. Quality and Curriculum Authority (QCA) (1998) *The Grammar Papers*. London: QCA, p. 55.

15. National Association for the Teaching of English (1997) *Position Paper: Grammar*, p. 2. NATE: Sheffield.

16. J. Williamson, and F. Hardman (1995) 'Time for refilling the bath? A study of primary student-teachers' grammatical knowledge', *Language and Education* **9**(2) 117–134.

17. G. Keith (1997) 'Teaching yourself English grammar', *The English and Media Magazine* **36**, (Summer) pp. 8–12.

18. G. Francis (1994) 'Grammar teaching in schools: what should teachers be aware of?', *Language Awareness* **3**(3) and **3**(4), p. 223.

19. M. Jones *et al.* (1996) *The Cheshire Cat*. Chester: Cheshire LEA.

20. M. Harris and K. Rowan (1989) 'Explaining grammatical concepts', *Journal of Basic Writing* **8**(2), pp. 21–41.

21. Language in the National Curriculum (LINC) (1992) *LINC Materials for Professional Development*. Nottingham: Department of English Studies, University of Nottingham, p. 352.

22. C. Weaver (1996) *Teaching Grammar in Context*. Portsmouth, NH: Boynton/Cook.

23. S. Peterson (1998) 'Teaching writing and grammar in context', in C. Weaver (ed.) *Lessons to Share on Teaching Grammar in Context*. Portsmouth, NH: Boynton/Cook, p. 77.

24. C. Weaver (ed.) (1998) *Lessons to Share on Teaching Grammar in Context*. Portsmouth, NH: Boynton/Cook, p. 26.

25. S. Peterson (1998) 'Teaching writing and grammar in context' in C. Weaver (ed.) *Lessons to Share on Teaching Grammar in Context*. Portsmouth, NH: Boynton/Cook, p. 75.

26. C. Weaver (1996) *Teaching Grammar in Context*. Portsmouth, NH: Boynton/Cook.

27. E. Gowers (1951) *ABC of Plain Words*. London: HMSO, pp. 2–3.

28. See, for example, C. Weaver (ed.) (1998) *Lessons to Share on Teaching Grammar in Context*. Portsmouth, NH: Boynton/Cook, pp. 28–30.

29. See, for example, E. Bearne (1998) *Making Progress in English*. London: Routledge, p. 206.

30. Cited in M. Sharples (1999) *How We Write:Writing as Creative Design*. London: Routledge, p. 39.

31. Nominalisation is discussed for example in K. Perera (1984) *Children's Writing and Reading*. Oxford: Blackwell, pp. 188–189 and 293–4, R. Bunting (1997) *Teaching about Language in the Primary Years*. London: David Fulton, p. 41 and G. Cook (1992) *Discourse of Advertising*. London: Routledge, p. 97.

32. See D. Crystal (1991) *Language A–Z for KS 3/4*. Harlow: Longman, p. 6–7; and D. Shiach (1998) *Grammar to 14*. Oxford: Oxford University Press, p. 22.

33. We are grateful to Sue Palmer for passing this on.
34. C. Weaver (ed.) (1998) *Lessons to Share on Teaching Grammar in Context*. Portsmouth, NH:Boynton/Cook, p. 24.
35. See the series of articles in *Primary English*, starting from No. 2, 1997. Other useful material is to be found in *The Cheshire Cat* (see note 19 above) and in G. Keith (1994) *Get the Grammar*. London: BBC.
36. D. Crystal (1996) *Discover Grammar*. Harlow: Longman.
37. *The Cambridge Encyclopaedia of the English Language* (1995) and *The Cambridge Encyclopaedia of Language* (1997). Gill Francis (see note 18 above) refers to another source of language data: *Cobuild* – the 'Bank of English – a large collection of natural language, indexed and stored on computer and accessible for interrogation'.
38. E. Bain, and R. Bain (1996) *The Grammar Book*. Sheffield: NATE, p. 6 and p. 114 makes useful suggestions about developing a 'language variety box' and using 'junk mail'.
39. *The Observer (Review)* 21 March, 1999, p. 11.
40. (1) GENERAL (noun, grammatical subject) FLIES (verb) then EITHER BACK (adverb) TO (preposition) FRONT (noun meaning 'foremost line of an army, nearest the enemy') OR BACK TO FRONT (adverb phrase meaning 'in reverse, in disorder). (2) An example of 'ellipsis' (omission of a word or words necessary to complete a sentence, something which is common in headlines to keep them short and snappy). Could mean . . . *more than EITHER boys do* (noun/verb) OR *they like boys* (pronoun/verb/noun-object etc). (8) (a) No commas around the subordinate or dependent clause 'who is French' makes it a 'restrictive' (sometimes called a 'defining') clause, so that the speaker *seems* to be making it clear that he is talking about his French wife rather than his Norwegian wife, his Russian wife, and so on! Providing the commas in (b) signals that it is a 'non-restrictive' (sometimes called a 'non-defining') clause: an additional but inessential piece of information.
41. Department for Education and Employment (DfEE) (1998) *The National Literacy Strategy: Framework for Teaching*. London: HMSO. (Teaching Grammar Through Shared and Guided Reading and Writing). DfEE (1998) advises: 'Colour-code different parts of speech to create sets of words on coloured cards, e.g. nouns on blue card, adjectives on red, adverbs on green . . .' Which colour for 'fast', for example?
42. In, respectively, S. Brownjohn and G. Gwyn-Jones (1996) *Spotlight on the English Language*. London: Hodder & Stoughton, pp. 30–31; and S. Hackman and C. Humphreys (1997) *Grammar and Punctuation 9–13*. London: Hodder & Stoughton, p. 74.
43. M. Sharples (1999) *How We Write: Writing as Creative Design*. London: Routledge, p. 20.

Further reading

Bain, E. and Bain, R. (1996) *The Grammar Book*. Sheffield: NATE.
Bain, R. and Bridgewood, M. (1998) *The Primary Grammar Book*. Sheffield: NATE.
Barton, G. (1997) *Grammar Essentials*. Harlow: Longman.
Crystal, D. (1996) *Discover Grammar*. Harlow: Longman.
Hackman, S. and Humphreys, C. (1997) *Grammar and Punctuation 9–13*. London: Hodder & Stoughton.
Hudson, R. (1992) *Teaching Grammar: a Guide for the National Curriculum*. Oxford: Blackwell.
Hurford, J. (1994) *Grammar: A Student's Guide*. Cambridge: Cambridge University Press.
Jones, M., Selby, J. *et al.* (1996) *The Cheshire Cat*. Chester: Cheshire Education Authority.
Keith, G. (1994) *Get the Grammar*. London: BBC.
Mason, M. (1999) *Knowledge about Language for Primary School Teachers: A Self-Access Course*. Wigan: Wigan and Leigh College.
Shiach, D. (1998) *Grammar to 14*. Oxford: Oxford University Press.
Smee, M. (1997) *Grammar Matters*. Oxford: Heinemann.
Wray, D. and Medwell, J. (1997) *English for Primary Teachers: An Audit and Self-Study Guide*. London: Letts.

Chapter 6
'Is this write?': learning to write and writing to learn

Mary Williams and Robert Fisher

Dear JPM WW HYP the L f Hannah (Hannah, aged 5)
(Dear Jolly Postman we will help you post the letters from Hannah.)

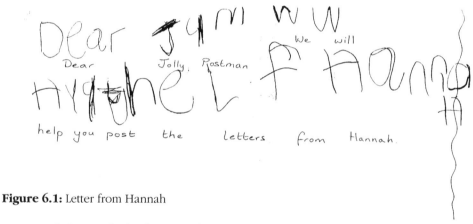

Figure 6.1: Letter from Hannah

Writing helps me think what I say. (Sophie, aged 8)

At one time, very little emphasis in writing was given to what young children wanted to 'say'. Writing in the early years of school was often little more than handwriting practise copied from the blackboard. However, researchers have found that children's earliest marks, as observed in preschool settings and the home, are both systematic and logical, as in Hannah's example in Figure 6.1, where a letter stands, for the most part, for a whole word. It seems that children develop hypotheses about the process which gradually emerge as they encounter written words in the world around them, most predominantly from books that are read to them. Among the assumptions they tend to make about the writing process is: that there is a minimum word length, i.e. that a word should have at least three letters (not one to which Hannah conforms); that there is a relationship between the size of the object they are writing about and the letters they use, e.g. an elephant would be written in large letter-like forms whereas a mouse would be written much smaller; or that length of word relates to the ages of the people involved, as with Mariana who decided that she has four letters in her name because she was four-year-old, whereas her father, whom she thought to be very old, has a thousand![1]

Developing writing in the early years

Children should have the opportunity to put their thoughts into writing from as young an age as possible, so that they can begin to make sense of the process for themselves. They should be given the chance to 'say' what they like in their writing as this will help them to develop a sense of authorship. As they engage in this they are likely to experiment with a number of principles which are integral to the process as well as growing in their understanding of the symbolic nature of writing and how this relates to the arrangement of letters and words on the page[2]. For example, Lisa, aged three years and nine months, demonstrated a recurring principle in her writing – that letters are made up of circles and lines – which she replicated with great care in her pattern-making by covering a strip of centimetre squared paper with a series of circles and downward strokes. Edward, aged four years, showed flexibility in his first attempt at writing his name, 'Ed2wrd', thinking, at this stage, that letters and numbers are interchangeable. (To fully appreciate the logic of his response you need to hear him say it aloud.)

Harshita at five years of age knows that writing is made up of shapes that are generated over and over again and uses the letters she is familiar with, i.e. those in her own name, as well as word-length squiggles to produce her writing. In addition, she is aware that print is permanent and was able to tell her teacher what her story, modelled on Alan Ahlberg's *Funny Bones*, was all about:

> Funny Bones went to the park and the dog skeleton
> bashed into a tree and it tipped over a park bench.
> Funny Bones never ever went there again.

In the following example Ben, aged six years, shows that he has not fully come to terms with the arrangement of letters and words on the page.

> I went to a spooky yard and a witch came out nad she cot me and
> dna tuo dpmuj I dna top nicoc a ni em tup ehs
> I went bak home

These examples also show how children's understanding of the conventions of writing grows with time and experience of print in the environment around them.

Developmental, emergent, process approaches such as these were endorsed in the first English National Curriculum (DES 1990) in which a 'growing mastery' of the process was recognised as important. This was derived from the recommendations in the earlier Cox Report[3] in which 'a measure of tolerance of errors' was advocated and seen to be positively useful for assessment purposes (Chapter 8) as a means of establishing a child's current state of knowledge and understanding.

Of equal importance is the fact that developmental approaches to learning to write do not conflict with the following widely accepted principles of education in the early years which underline how:

- Learning can be achieved through discovery and play.
- Assessment of progress should be based on what children can do, rather than what they cannot do.

As with other aspects of learning, experimentation through play[4] will increase young children's knowledge, skills and understanding of the writing learning process. So it is important that teaching approaches adopted for four-year-olds in reception classes are not too formal. Preschool aged children should be encouraged to 'use pictures, symbols, familar words and letters, to communicate meaning, showing awareness of some of the different purposes of writing[5] as outlined for the reception year of the National Literacy Strategy (DfEE 1998a) in which it is stated that they should 'use writing to communicate in a variety of ways, incorporating it into play and everyday classroom life'[6].

Table 6.1 shows how approaches to teaching writing in the reception year (4/5 years) mirror what is known about the stages the young child goes through as an 'emergent writer'.

Emergent skills of the young writer	Learning objectives in the reception year (DfEE 1998a)
Knows which is their drawing and which is their writing.	Distinguishes between writing and drawing.
Understands the permanent nature of written language.	Knows that words can be written down to be read again for a wide range of purposes. Understands that writing remains constant i.e. will always 'say' the same thing.
Invents spellings starting with a '3 letter' hypothesis. Develops increased phonetic regularity and accuracy in orthographic spelling. conventional	Invents spellings derived from phonic analogy making. Experiments with writing and recognises how their own version matches and differs from the form.
Uses own name as the base for experimentation with the writing process.	Writes own name and explores others words related to the spelling of own name.
Understands concepts of directionality in writing.	Knows that words are ordered from left to right and that they need to be read in this way to make sense. Tracks the text in the right order – left to right. Understands how writing is formed directionally.

Table 6.1: Emergent Writing and the National Literacy Strategy

Early writing and the Literacy Hour

Teachers need to resist pressure for over-formalisation of the early years curriculum and to stand firm in what is known to be right for young children. Equally, because of all the competing demands on time they will need to be creative in teaching through the Literacy Hour. Children need to be offered more than just time to play as play can so easily become unchallenging if they are left to their own devices[7]. What is needed is for an adult, either a teacher, a nursery nurse or a classroom helper, to play alongside them in order to model aspects of the writing process, for example in the context of a home corner theme such as Postman Pat's post office (p. 82) or 'Three Bears' cottage (see below for an example of a writing task on the theme of the Three Bears). If the home corner is set up to reflect in some way the theme of the book being used for shared reading within the Literacy Hour then what is being learned can be reinforced. It is essential that shared sessions in reading and writing retain the interest of the child so they need to vary in format as young children so easily become bored. This view was confirmed by one able child, already capable of writing her own poetry, who responded with a sigh when asked what she thought about the Literacy Hour: 'On Monday you have a Big Book and you read it again and again, and on the next Monday you have another Big Book and you read it again and again!' (Katie, aged 5)

Young children need to hear stories read from the beginning to the end in order to experience fully 'being taken into other worlds' (Meek 1991). Without time being given to this, they are unlikely to find their own 'voice' in writing. Equally, teachers need to model writing across a range of genres such as daily plans, shopping lists or written instructions, to increase and broaden children's understanding of the writing process. To avoid a sense of frustration like Katie's it is essential that a flexible approach to the Literacy Hour is adopted. This is most easily achieved if several texts relating to a single theme are included each week but from which it is possible to develop understanding and skills at word, sentence and text level as advocated in the termly objectives for the particular age group.

Example of a Key Stage 1 stimulus for writing

As part of a series of Literacy Hour lessons based on the 'Three Bears' story select a range of books which relate to this theme including relevant extracts from fiction and information books about bears.

In one lesson, as part of 'shared reading' read the children the letter from the *The Jolly Postman or Other People's Letters*[8] which Goldilocks sends by way of apology for the havoc she has wreaked in the three bears household. Then ask a focus group under guided writing to compose the letter which initiated this response, i.e. a letter of complaint from Father Bear and Mother Bear. This activity involves children in 'higher order thinking' in that they have to analyse and synthesise what they know about the story from the various sources on offer in order to assess how the aggrieved parents of baby bear would feel.

Figure 6.2 is the first draft of a response from an able six-year-old in which he shows considerable awareness of his audience.

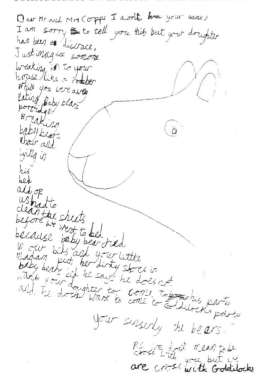

Dear Mr and Mrs Copps I don't know your name,
I am sorry to tell you this but your daughter
has been a discrace.
Just imagine someone
breaking in to your
house like a robber
while you were away
eating Baby bears
porridge.
Breaking
baby bears
chair and
lying in
his
bed
all of
us had to
clean the sheets
before we went to bed
because baby bear cried
in our beds and your little
madam put her dirty shoes in
baby bears bed he says he does not
want your daughter to come to his party
and he doesn't want to come to Goldilocks party
yours sinserely the bears.
P.S. we dont mean to be
cross with you but we
are cross with Goldilocks

Figure 6.2: Letter from 'The Bears'

This lesson could also used to develop and assess spelling ability – word level work – as the children could be asked to act as Goldilocks' teacher who is going to correct the spelling mistakes she has made in her letter to the three bears; or to work as response partners to help each other edit the first drafts of their own letters (see above). Children should be encouraged, at least, to underline words which are spelled incorrectly even if they do not know what the correct form is yet.

By these means, in National Literacy Strategy terms, work at:

- text level: developing composition styles appropriate to audience and purpose
- sentence level: developing an understanding of sentence construction and punctuation
- word level: developing spelling, vocabulary and handwriting

will have been undertaken.

Developing a range of writing

What kind of writing are we doing today? (Sean, aged 7)

In the past the form of writing that dominated teaching in schools was that of story but as children's writing ability develops they need to have their repertoire broadened. During Key Stage 1 they should be introduced to other forms of writing such as signs, labels, captions, lists, instructions, recounts, non-chronological reports and, building on this in Key Stage 2, they should learn how to proceed, report, argue, persuade, explain and discuss in their writing (DfEE 1998a). The advantage of beginning with story writing is that it mirrors more closely the habits of spoken speech than does non-fiction writing. We dream, gossip and make sense of the world through stories. However, written stories are not the same as spoken stories. With speech, it is possible to convey subtle meanings through intonation, facial expression or gesture, whereas in writing this is much more difficult. With speech, immediate feedback is given so the message can be altered accordingly by explaining points further, repeating certain words or phrases and so on. With writing, feedback may be offered some time later or sometimes not at all. With speech, others have to prompt us into further utterance or explanation. There is no prompting between a writer and a sheet of paper so teachers have a key role to bridge this gap by challenging children to put their meaning across effectively.

Writing a text, whether story or non-fiction, provides the child with the most complex of intellectual and physical challenges. If the writing is by hand, not only must the child manipulate pen or pencil in skilful, regular, abstract patterns but they must get spelling, grammar (syntax) and style right in order to give meaning to others (semantics). To maintain sense in a passage, children need to master complex cohesive devices to help keep 'the thread' of meaning, for example in the use of pronouns for nouns.

With non-fiction writing, children have to develop their skills even further which can be even more challenging as technical vocabulary and more formal and impersonal registers are used. Non-fiction is organised in a variety of ways, and these need to be learned. Recent research has shown how both reading and writing can be enhanced through familiarity with non-fiction genres, in particular by introducing children to different forms of factual and non-narrative writing[9]. The term 'genre' is used to identify the different forms which texts can take according to the social purposes they serve. As children emerge as writers they need to learn how to apply their skills across a range of genres of writing. They need to be introduced to different aspects of the writing process whatever the form of their writing. The range of features they need to learn and think about includes:

Features	Questions to consider
Purpose	Why are we writing this? What other reasons are there for writing?
Audience	Who are we writing this for? Who else might we be writing for?
Style and form	What kind of writing is this? What other kinds of writing are there?

Purpose

Through reading and being read to from a wide range of different genres children will become aware of the way style differs according to the purpose of the text. However, they will not just pick this up for themselves. Teachers need to help them to develop understanding of the purposes of writing. Three broad purposes for writing might be identified as:

- personal – writing for yourself, e.g. personal notes, diary, letters
- imaginative – writing for others, e.g. stories, poems, plays
- functional – writing for a practical purpose, e.g. recipes, instructions, information.

One way of developing this understanding is to ask children to explain the qualities they would expect to see in different kinds of writing. For example what do they think the differences are between personal, imaginative and functional writing?

The following are qualities in different forms of writing as identified by a Year 4 class (8–9-year-olds):

Personal writing

- 'You use it when you know someone well.'
- 'It is about your personal life.'
- 'The word 'I' is used.'
- 'The word 'we' is used.'
- 'It is about you not anyone else.'
- 'It tells about your thoughts and feelings.'
- 'You are speaking to yourself.'

Imaginative writing

- 'It is not real.'
- 'It is an untrue story, for example about dinosaurs.'
- 'It uses interesting words.'
- 'It's made up in your head.'
- 'You can see pictures in your head.'
- 'It is made up, not true.'
- 'It can be funny or scary.'

Functional writing

- 'It tells you how to do things.'
- 'It gives information about things.'
- 'It is serious.'
- 'It is not real or made up.'
- 'It can tell you things you don't know.'
- 'It gives you advice about what to do.'

Children also need to know that the same piece of writing can fulfil different functions. For example, an e-mail can be personal, imaginative and functional at the same time. They can be given different pieces of writing to sort and discuss what kind or type of writing they think each piece is. 'Why are we writing this?' or 'Why has this been written?' are questions that can be asked about any piece of writing. Another question to ask is 'Who is it written for?'

Audience

In the early stages, children's audience for writing is likely to be either themselves or known recipients such as parents/carers, and, possibly at a later date, their teachers. They need to know that writing for unknown audiences places certain demands on a writer in terms of establishing the context, explaining terms and spelling out relationships. Children need to be aware of the needs of their audience and to anticipate problems in understanding which might occur as they write. Audiences are not of course limited to time and place. They might be writing for distant and unknown audiences, as on the Internet.

Our research shows that many children do not know, or find it difficult to say, who they are writing for[10]. As Sonal, aged six, said: 'I don't know who it's for, you just write what your teacher says,' whereas Claire, whose writing was going to be included on her school's Web site, certainly knew who she was writing for: 'I am sending this to everyone in the world.'

It is important, therefore, to discuss with children the possible audiences they might be writing for, and to give them experience of writing for those which are both known or unknown to them:

Type of audience	*Known/unknown*
Self	known
Parent	known
Teacher/other pupils/friends	known
Other teachers/classes	partially known
Family members	partially known
Children in other schools/pen pals/Internet connections	unknown
The media/councillors/local businesses/community	unknown

Style and form

Recent research has shown how both reading and writing can be enhanced through non-fiction genres, in particular through introducing children to different forms of factual and non-narrative writing[11]. 'Genre' can be further defined as types of text whose form varies according to the purpose it serves. For example, early genres that children experience could include labels, stories and nursery rhymes. Fictional genres include fiction, poetry and plays. Non-fiction genres identified in the National Literacy Strategy are recount (past tense), report (present tense), explanation, procedural (such as a recipe), persuasion (argument) and discussion (arguments from different viewpoints, as in the persuasion writing frame in Figure 6.3 on p.75).

Non-narrative factual forms have been neglected in the past and are still causing problems in terms of children's learning through writing (QCA 1998). The range of writing children experience in school needs to be extended to include both story forms and non-narrative types of writing such as:

- letters
- descriptions
- reviews
- reports
- instructions
- explanations
- arguments.

The following are some writing activities planned by a teacher to link to a story about mice she was studying with her class:

- Write a letter from a mouse to a person who is scared of mice, telling them why they should not be afraid. (persuasion)
- Write a description of a mouse to match an illustration. (description)
- Write a review of two books about mice saying which you prefer and why. (review)
- Make a scrapbook of information about mice using material from books and the Internet. (report)
- Write instructions on how to care for a mouse. (instruction)
- Design a mouse trap and explain how it should be made and used. (explanation)
- Write arguments to persuade someone why you would rather be a country (or town) mouse. (argument)

One way to generate non-narrative writing is to pose a problem. When a real problem is posed, for example: 'What is air?', the children can be asked to think about it for themselves initially, then discuss it in pairs and then share ideas with the group or class. This process of 'think-pair-share' can provide the important oral groundwork of accessing prior knowledge and sharing ideas that will later be the basis for writing. Information can then be gathered from a range of relevant books and recorded in a manner suitable to the subject, including the use of computer resources and ICT (see Chapter 9).

Matching 'style to audience and purpose' can be taught not only through the shared reading and writing aspects of the Literacy Hour but also through other encounters with print. These take place across the whole curriculum as children use information books to extend their knowledge and understanding, e.g. in history and science. Every opportunity should be taken to discuss with children the key features of a broad range of texts. They should be questioned about the effectiveness of a particular author's style during shared and guided reading. In shared writing, teachers should try to model, through 'thinking aloud', what needs to be considered when using a particular style for writing, bearing in mind the needs of an intended audience. During such sessions the teacher can act as a scribe for children's (or their own) ideas in order to demonstrate what real writers do during the act of creating words on paper or on a computer screen. As one teacher commented: 'I should not expect my children to write if I have not shown them again and again what to do and how to do it.'

Extending writing within the Literacy Hour

The 'shared' aspect of the Literacy Hour provides an ideal opportunity for teachers to model aspects of the writing process. There are several ways that this can be achieved. The first is modelling, in which the teacher discusses during a shared reading the uses and features of the genre of text being read. The second is the joint creation of a written text with the children, based on the genre or a theme from a text being used (as in the Three Bears example above) during shared or guided writing. Here the teacher shares information about the features of the genre and models the sorts of questions that skilled writers ask themselves (e.g. as listed above) as they write. During group or independent time the children can go on to construct new texts in the same genre, both drafting and editing the text in consultation with peers, prior to final publication and evaluation in a debriefing or plenary session. The cycle should be repeated on increasingly more challenging aspects of genre. Research shows that this model has been found to be most helpful in supporting children's development as writers and is a characteristic of 'effective teachers of literacy'[12].

You might consider turning a Literacy Hour into a 'writer's workshop' focusing on either fiction or non-fiction writing. During the hour this might include:

- sharing and discussing with pupils examples of how one or more writers have dealt with a theme or issue in writing
- asking pupils to compose for themselves during shared writing time, while you write down the children's ideas
- giving pupils twenty minutes to write for themselves, while you concentrate on helping one focus group of writers
- reassembling the class in the plenary ten minutes to share and review, identifying what is good about each piece of writing and how it might be improved.

In writing fiction focus on one or more aspects of the writer's art, for example, the plot (theme or genre), narrative structure (especially good beginnings and endings), interesting characters, evocative settings, and use of dialogue.

The following are ten tips from teachers to help children write stories in a short time:

Writing short stories

1. Use only one or two main characters.
2. Plan a good beginning to capture the reader's interest, but keep it short.
3. The main part is the 'middle', then move the problem quickly on to a resolution.
4. Describe the setting, and any changes within it as the story goes along.
5. Tell your reader how characters think and feel.
6. Make characters talk about what is happening (but don't always use the word 'said').
7. Use a variety of sentence lengths, and avoid repetition of words, e.g. at start of sentences.
8. Finish the story with a good last line or sentence.
9. As you write, read the story through to yourself to see if it makes sense.
10. Finish with five minutes to spare, to check your draft for punctuation and spelling.

An effective strategy to help children in writing either fiction or non-fiction is through the use of 'writing frames'. This is another scaffolding approach which can help support young writers by giving starters and key questions to help prompt and structure their writing and to bridge any gaps in understanding[13]. Figure 6.3 is an example of a writing frame which helped Year 4 children to structure their arguments into a discussion for and against whether children should wear school uniform.

Composition and transcription: finding a balance

One of the possible weaknesses of the Literacy Hour is that the time allowed for independent or group work (twenty minutes) is insufficient for children to engage in extended pieces of writing[14]. This concern is linked to the problem of deciding how much attention should be given to the composition or transcription aspects of the process. The problem is best solved by taking a balanced approach, viewing both these elements as mutually dependent and, therefore, to be given equal attention. When there is a balance between composing and transcription children are encouraged to express their thoughts and feelings on a wide variety of subjects which are meaningful to

Name:	*Jane Brewster*		
Title:	*Should children wear school uniform?*		

Make notes in the boxes below listing arguments for and against.

Arguments for	Arguments against
1. There is not the problem of parents not knowing what to buy their children for school.	1. Children cannot choose what to wear for school, everyone has to have the same.
2. School uniform makes you feel proud of going to your school.	2. School uniform is expensive. Some parents can't afford it and have to get it from second-hand shops.
3. You know who goes to your school if they are wearing the uniform.	3. School uniforms can be boring and muddy colours.
4. Some children get way out ideas about fashon (sic) and everyone copies them.	4. If your school uniform is in the wash in the morning youve (sic) got trouble!
5. School uniform makes you look smart.	5. You can choose comfortable clothes for yourself.

My conclusion based on these arguments is
I think children should be allowed to choose whether they wear school uniform or not
because
there are arguments for both sides.

Figure 6.3: Writing frame for an argument or discussion completed by a nine-year-old

them in appropriate styles for their intended purpose. To achieve this children need to:

- be motivated in terms of subject material, using books and stories as the impetus, during text level work, as a means of helping them to find their own voice in their writing
- be taught to write legibly and use spelling, grammar and punctuation accurately
- be shown how to plan, draft, revise and edit their writing
- be supported in the writing process by the use of a 'response friend', writing group or teacher to help improve their writing
- be given sufficient time to complete extended pieces of writing
- be encouraged to share, judge and evaluate their writing and the writing of others.

Some teachers have found it helpful to post advice on the process of writing and responding to writing, such as these reminders to a class of ten-year-olds:

When you have drafted your writing:
1. Read it aloud to yourself.
2. Ask yourself, 'Is there anything I want to add or change?'
3. Read your writing to a 'response friend'.
4. Ask if he/she has any good ideas to improve your writing.
5. Give your revised draft to an adult to read.

How to be a good 'response friend'
1. Listen carefully to your friend read his/her work.
2. Tell your friend what you liked about the writing.
3. Think how it might be improved – Will the audience understand it?
   Will they find it interesting?
   Is there anything missing?
   Can you suggest any words or changes?
   Is it the right length?
4. Suggest how the writing might be improved.

Acting as a 'response friend' will help children to gain awareness or metacognitive understanding of the writing process through discussing features of composition and transcription to help their partner to improve a real piece of writing. It helps children to engage with the question that is a challenge for every teacher: 'How do you help someone to improve their writing?'

Shared reading and textual analysis of samples of writing with children, can enhance their understanding of the process of writing and what it means to be a good writer. Discussion of writing between the child, or group of children, and a teacher (or conferencing, as it is sometimes called) will help to develop a shared vocabulary for discussing writing[15]. Such discussions should help older children become familar with the technical language of English including the use of grammatical terms (Chapter 5), as well as important textual features such as cohesion, voice, style and the use of imagery.

Another approach is to involve children in assessing writing, and in particular to discuss the criteria used for judging a good piece of writing. The box below gives some criteria brainstormed by Year 4 children and their teacher.

What makes a good piece of writing?

Children	Teacher
'be a good story'	Understanding of story (or genre) structure: e.g. a story should have a good: – beginning (setting the scene, interesting the reader) – development (interesting events/characters/problems) – resolution (ending where the problem/problems are resolved)
'have good words'	Use of vocabulary: Writing should be expressed in 'best words' e.g. use of imaginative expressions for detail and description – range of adjectives, verbs, adverbs – expanded noun phrases e.g. 'One cold, frosty morning . . .'
'explain things well'	Use of stylistic features: Writing should have a good style e.g. through use of – varied sentences, short and expanded – metaphor and simile – repetition and alliteration
'make sense'	Use of Standard English: e.g. use correct written forms of expression, including – range of appropriate connecting words to extend sentences – correct use of punctuation and spelling – consistent use of tenses
'be interesting to read'	Awareness of the needs of the reader: e.g. written with audience and purpose in mind, including interesting content that is well paced/sequenced

Other questions that can challenge children (as well as us their teachers) to think about and articulate their understanding of writing include:

- 'What five hints would you give a younger child to help them become a good writer?'
- 'Why is it good for children to learn to write?'
- 'What must you do to improve your writing?'

Part of the value of writing is that it enables us to think about our own thinking. Writing can help develop metacognitive awareness at three levels:

- knowledge of task: what is the writing task – its form, audience, and purpose?
- knowledge of process: what do you do – draft, revise, edit, share?
- knowledge of self: what kind of writer are you – what helps you to write well?

But to give the last word to a child. Here Tom, aged ten, explains what the writing process means to him:

> When I write I find it easier at first to discuss my ideas with others, then have a go. I like to think what to write about without rushing into it. I prefer to write in rough first, because I can change things. I wrote this in rough first. Then I can make it better by changing things. I change things like boring words to unboring words or my lines if they are too long. I don't like too much noise when I write so I can hear myself think. I like to write a lot of ideas and only keep the ones (sic) that are good, so it makes sense and sounds right. I then read it through and check for spelling mistakes. Sometimes it helps to discuss what you are writing with a friend. When I give it in I hope the teacher will say 'good work'.

Notes

1. E. Ferreiro and A. Teberosky (1979), researching in Argentina, showed that children's emergent mark-making was not merely haphazard scribbling as once had been thought.
2. Marie Clay (1972) showed through research that children did not automatically acquire 'concepts about print' such as directionality, letter and word concepts, book orientation and punctuation but needed them taught explicitly. Nigel Hall (1987) and A. Browne (1995) have investigated further the principles children adhere to as they emerge as writers.
3. These approaches in the English National Curriculum (DES 1990) were derived from recommendations in the earlier Cox Report (1989, 10.8).
4. T. Bruce (1991), C. Nutbrown (1994) and T. David (1998) have identified from research key principles in effective teaching of young children, in particular the importance of structured play in the early years.
5. *Desirable Outcomes for Children's Learning* (DfEE 1996) were laid down for children under five in nursery and reception classes in schools in England and Wales. Further guidance can be found in the *Early Learning Goals* (DfEE 1999c).
6. National Literacy Strategy (DfEE 1998a, p. 19). Similarly, in the first draft of the 'new' English curriculum there is endorsement of developmental principles, for example, in the statement that '*during* the key stage they [pupils] should become independent writers of texts which are correctly spelled, with sentences punctuated correctly'. (DfEE, December 1999, p. 5).
7. C. Meadows and A. Cashdan (1988) were influential in showing that adults need to engage in meaningful dialogue with children if the learning opportunities afforded by play are to be maximised.
8. Based on Janet and Allan Ahlberg (1986) *The Jolly Postman or Other People's Letters*. London: Heinemann.
9. R. Beard (1999) offers a useful review of research related to writing in the National Literacy Strategy. J. R. Martin (1989) outlines and discusses the important role of factual writing.

10. Williams, M. and Fisher, R. (1998) *Brunel Research Into Literacy* (unpublished).
11. See D. Wray and M. Lewis (1997) *Extending Literacy: Children Reading and Writing Non-fiction* (Routledge), which draws extensively on the Exeter Extending Literacy (EXEL) project. Wray and Lewis's work in turn strongly influenced the emphasis on using non-fiction in the National Literacy Strategy (DfEE 1998a).
12. J. Medwell *et al.* (1998) in a report for the Teacher Training Agency aimed at identifying the characteristics of effective teachers of literacy.
13. D. Wray and M. Lewis (1997) offer approaches to 'scaffolding' writing based on the earlier theories of L. Vygotsky (1962) and J. Bruner (1983).
14. M. Williams (1999) researched the dissemination of the National Literacy Strategy policy and its effect on practice in primary classrooms from the perspective of student teachers (unpublished) and this was a critical feature relating to writing at Key Stage 2.
15. For example, in the 'Framework of Objectives' (National Literacy Strategy, DfEE 1998a, p. 22) by Term 2 of Year 1, pupils are expected 'to use the term sentence appropriately to identify sentences in the text' although explicit reference to this sort of knowledge ceases by Year 4, Term 3. It must therefore be supposed that children should be familar with the technical language of English by then.

Further reading

Beard, R. (1999) *National Literacy Strategy: Review of Research and Related Evidence.* London: DfEE.

Browne, A. (1995) *Developing Language and Literacy.* London: Paul Chapman Publishing.

Bruce, T. (1991) *Time to Play.* London: Hodder & Stoughton.

Clay, M. (1972) *Reading: The Patterning of Complex Behaviour*, 2nd edn. London: Heinemann.

David, T. (1998) 'Learning properly! Young children and desirable outcomes', *Journal of the Professional Association of Early Childhood Educators* **18**(2), Spring, 1998.

DES (1988) *English for Ages 5 to 11.* London: HMSO.

DES (1990) *English in the National Curriculum (No.2).* London: HMSO.

DfEE (1996) *Desirable Outcomes for Children's Learning.* London: HMSO.

DfEE (1998a) *The National Literacy Strategy: Framework for Teaching.* London: HMSO.

DfEE (1998b) *Teachers Meeting the Challenge of Change.* Green Paper.

DfEE (1999a) *English in the National Curriculum.* London: HMSO.

DfEE (1999b) *The Review of the National Curriculum in England.* London: HMSO.

DfEE (1999c) *Early Learning Goals.* London: QCA Publications.

Ferreiro, E. and Teberosky, A. (1979) *Literacy Before Schooling.* London: Heinemann.

Hall, N. (1987) *The Emergence of Literacy.* London: Hodder & Stoughton.

Martin, J. R. (1989) *Factual Writing: Exploring and Challenging Social Reality.* Oxford: Oxford University Press.

Meek, M. (1991) *On Being Literate.* London: Bodley Head.

Meadows, C. and Cashdan, A. (1988) *Helping Children Learn.* London: David Fulton Publishers.

Medwell, J. *et al.* (1998) *Effective Teachers of Literacy: A Report of a Research Project Commissioned by the Teacher Training Agency.* Exeter: School of Education.

Nutbrown, C. (1994) *Threads of Thinking.* London: Paul Chapman.

QCA (1998) *Standards at Key Stage 2: English, Mathematics and Science: Report on the 1998 National Curriculum Assessments for 11-Year-Olds.* London: QCA Publications.

QCA (1999) *QCA's Work In Progress to Develop the School Curriculum.* London: QCA Publications.

Williams, M. (1998) *A Study which Explores the Impact of the English National Curriculum (1990) on the Work of Teachers at Key Stage 2.* PhD Thesis (unpublished), Brunel University.

Wray, D. and Lewis, M. (1997) *Extending Literacy: Children Reading and Writing Non-fiction.* London: Routledge.

Chapter 7
'What did I say?': speaking, listening and drama

Colleen Johnson

Aiden: 'Miss, are we doing drama after play?'
Teacher: 'We certainly are.'
Class 4J: 'Yesss!'

It was the start of playtime and already the children were looking forward to coming back into the classroom to get on with their work. As teachers, we know the importance of motivation in learning. Children are often highly inspired by their involvement in both creating and reflecting upon drama. Fleming suggests that 'drama's motivational force . . . harnesses the inclination to play . . .'[1]. If this inclination can be used to promote learning, then a powerful argument for the place of drama in the primary curriculum is offered. In this chapter I will consider some of the ways in which the subject can enhance children's learning, specifically in relation to literacy. The drama strategies used do not require specialist knowledge and the activities described illustrate ways in which drama can help teachers realise the objectives of the National Literacy Strategy.

Why drama?

Drama is an art form in itself. All primary school children participate in dramatic performance: for example, by taking part in and watching 'assemblies' and plays and by visiting the theatre and taking part in theatre-in-education visits to the school. Most see drama daily on television, following soaps such as 'Hollyoaks', written specifically for a young audience. Children enjoy talking about what they have 'seen on television the night before'.

Drama is a learning medium through which children can explore concepts and acquire knowledge and understanding. For example to recreate historical events by working in role as archaeologists, identifying artefacts to discover more about how certain people lived, or as scientists conducting experiments on 'samples from the moon' as a means of learning more about minerals.

Drama is unique in that it enables teachers and children to create an unlimited variety of contexts: from the inside of the giant's castle at the top of the beanstalk to the Frank family's secret attic in Amsterdam; from the village post office to a space station on Mars. Children can explore these imagined worlds from within by engaging actively with specific aspects of a story or situation. They do this by empathising with the characters involved and exploring human behaviour in dilemmas which may well be beyond their own experiences, while being able to make connections with their own lives. Making these connections demands perception, imagination and interpretation[2]. By engaging in a dramatic situation, and then, out of role, reflecting upon that situation, the teacher and children are involved in a metacognitive process of imaginative thinking both individually and collectively. Such experiences enhance learning across all areas of the primary curriculum. However, the focus of this chapter will be the role of drama in the teaching of literacy. Through drama we can create different contexts in which children experience diversity in language and through these experiences develop confidence in their own use of, and knowledge about, language. Such experiences enhance all language learning, including Standard English and Language Study.

Drama, language and literacy

> Good oral work enhances pupils' understanding of language in both oral and written forms and of the way language can be used to communicate. (National Literacy Strategy, DfEE 1998)

The relationship between oracy (speaking and listening) and literacy (reading and writing) is central to language and literacy teaching. Talk is at the core of learning. The National Curriculum for Speaking and Listening refers to developing talk for different purposes and audiences. When a teacher uses drama to create contexts for talk, the range of contexts, purposes and situations is without limit and the wide range of types of talk required will challenge children's creative use of language.

Drama can give a purpose to reading and writing, requiring the children to interrogate, respond to and generate text. Having been engaged in dramatic activity to explore an aspect of a story aimed at predicting 'what comes next', children are encouraged to 'read on' in order to find out how their predictions match up with those of the writer. In addition, to develop understanding of a text written to be performed, children should have the opportunity to experience the text through performance, both their own and that of others.

The National Literacy Strategy advocates whole-class, group and individual teaching which engages pupils in active learning. Drama can stimulate the best in whole-class teaching through discursive and interactive talk, fostered and modelled by the teacher, for example during shared text work and the plenary session of the Literacy Hour. Good quality independent group work can be maintained when such talk continues while the children are working without teacher support. Through drama, the teacher can create the context for exploratory talk, developing children's confidence in the expression of hypothesis and opinion.

Teaching strategies

All of the approaches to drama work described in this chapter took place in the *classroom*. This is particularly advantageous in schools where space is at a premium and it is difficult to have access to larger spaces such as the gym or hall for lessons other than PE. In addition, a drama activity which may not demand more than a few minutes can be highly beneficial in stimulating further reading or written work. In this case, it is useful for the children to have near at hand the resources they will need, such as pens and books, and to be able to get to work immediately at their tables.

Still image

This strategy requires children to organise themselves into creating a three-dimensional image to represent a dramatic moment or a visual 'summing up' of a situation. Children are already familiar with the convention of the still image under many guises: for example, a pause on a video is a 'freeze frame', or they may have played 'musical statues', or sequenced a story using cartoon strips and added captions to 'snapshots'. (See also the use of 'still image' on p. 34)

For the teacher with little or no experience of drama, this is one of the most accessible approaches. It is useful as a control device, as a point of focus at the start of a lesson when recapping what has gone on before and as a safe way of presenting a moment of aggression or violence in a story, for example, the moment in Shakespeare's *Macbeth* when the hero is slain by Macduff. It enables the teacher to 'slow down' the pace of a narrative and examine a key incident in detail. It does not require a lot of space, nor is it usually a 'noisy' activity. It is immediate and, because of a limitation of time, the children must work quickly and with concentration.

A Year 3 class had been reading a story about Krishna and the Hydra, where a young boy saved a village from the sea monster by dancing on its many heads. The teacher stopped reading the story at the moment when Krishna walked to the water's edge, watched by the villagers.

Teacher: 'If we could put a picture in the book to illustrate this scene, what would it look like?'

One child volunteered to be Krishna and came to stand at the front, in the middle, facing toward the class. One by one, children put up their hands to join the image. After each had taken her or his place, the teacher asked the children to look at the image to see how it was changing and to think about where they might put themselves within it. She 'froze' the image once seven or eight children were in place. Then she introduced a second drama strategy.

Thought tracking

The teacher invited those in the still image to contribute the thoughts of the characters they were representing, one at a time:

Teacher: 'At that moment I thought to myself . . .'

She moved around the image, touching each child on the shoulder, inviting them to speak:

First villager: 'He must be mad!'
Second villager: 'He'll be eaten up!'
Krishna: 'It's now or never.'

Another way of combining these strategies would be to have those in the audience volunteer the thoughts of individuals already in the image. This makes an already active learning situation even more interactive. Additionally, the audience could be asked to invent a caption to go with the image, as those watching are in the best place to do this as they see the complete picture.

The teacher went one step further with this strategy. She asked all the children, those *in* role and those *out of* role, in turn, to predict what might happen next[3]. The predictions of those in the still image – most said that Krishna would perish – were considerably gloomier than those of the children watching. The teacher invited the children, *out of role*, to consider why this might be so. Discussion focused upon the children knowing that stories about Krishna as a child always ended happily because 'we know he grew up to be a god, so he must have been OK'. *Out of role*, the children knew that all would end happily. *In role*, however, as the villagers, the children experienced the immediacy of the moment when lives were held in the balance. As the thought-tracking exercise had shown, most of the 'villagers' had no confidence in the ability of a young boy to defeat a powerful monster.

The still image approach, once modelled by the teacher with the whole class, is useful for children to use for themselves independently of the teacher. For example, children in groups can be asked to choose the most significant part of a chapter in a story and then to create a still image to represent this, to present to the rest of the class. This involves highly focused discussion as the children negotiate meaning, and how to convey their interpretation to an audience[4]. It is more fruitful, and less time-consuming, to have an image to interpret than a short improvisation as children have been required to 'crystallise to the essence'[5] the significant moments of the narrative. The image created by a group will represent two things: a key moment or event and the quality of learning achievable through exploratory talk.

The teacher could use the still image to stimulate collaborative written work, for example, by asking children to write a short piece of dialogue suggested by the image produced. In this case, it would be helpful to have the children's chairs set up in a 'double horseshoe' arrangement. Two rows of chairs are placed in the shape of a horseshoe, with desks between them, leaving a space in the middle for 'performance'. When the children are required to work in pairs, the children on the front row turn around and work with those behind.

Teacher and children in role

The range of questioning which a teacher is able to use is significantly expanded if the teacher uses the strategy of working *in role*. In a Year 1 classroom, to support a theme of shops, services and dealing with money, the role-play area was set up as a post office with stationery, stamps, receipts, TV licences and a till with money. The children were involved in the sorts of activities which they may have observed in High Street post offices and other shops. They were highly motivated by having 'real' objects with which to work. A context for the role play itself was established where the children were already happily playing spontaneously. The teacher was watching a small group at work and after a while entered the post office as a customer:

Teacher: 'Can you help me? I need to send a letter to India.'

The 'counter assistants' furnished her with an air mail letter.

Teacher: 'This envelope is different to those [pointing to ordinary weight stationery]. Why is that?'

Some assistants talked about the need for air mail stationery to be lighter than that for surface mail, identifying the colour (usually blue) with stripes. They discussed the cost in relation to weight.

Teacher: 'Why is it more expensive to send a letter abroad?'

The assistants may already have the answer, or, with careful questioning, the teacher can develop their reasoning and help them to make the connection between transporting something by plane, which would suggest long distance travel, the number of people involved in the process and so on. To continue:

Teacher: 'Can you help me read my list? I've left my glasses at home.'

An assistant reads the list out loud. Other activities which are taking place in the 'post office', exploiting opportunities for literacy and numeracy, include letter writing, stocktaking, having to write an order for more stock and sorting and redirecting mail.

By intervening in role the teacher gained the opportunity both to assess and extend the pupils' learning by:

- Questioning the children to assess their current state of understanding.
- Giving them opportunities to use subject-specific language, such as lighter/heavier, cheaper/dearer, even subtotal/total.
- Scaffolding their understanding (as in the questioning about the cost of sending mail abroad).
- Differentiating, supporting and extending the children's understanding where appropriate.
- Giving a purpose to reading and writing in the role-play area and even adding a sense of ugency with her 'time limit'.

Teachers do not need to spend much time playing in role but brief interventions such as these can serve to increase the quality of the play and the learning which is derived from it.

Hot seating

This activity usually takes place with the children seated on the floor with one or two chairs placed in front of them, as in the Literacy Hour.

A Year 2 class had been reading a version of the story of 'Goldilocks and the Three Bears'. The teacher asked the children if they would like to interrogate Goldilocks about her visit to the Bears' home. She could have played the part herself as *teacher in role* but instead asked a for a volunteer to play Goldilocks who would sit on a centrally placed chair, or the *hot seat*. The children questioned Goldilocks about her actions, what her intentions had been and what she felt about the distress she had caused.

There are several variations to this technique which can be chosen to fit the levels of confidence of particular groups of children. The teacher can begin, as Goldilocks, to help establish the role and then can ask for a child to take over the role. After a short while, the teacher can swap another child into the role and onto the *hot seat*. This adds to the level of interaction, can help keep the drama from flagging while relieving any one child of the pressure of having to maintain the role for too long. There may be two or more *hot seats* with more characters, for example in this case, Goldilocks and her mother, as responses from one character may elicit a question from the children for the other. The *hot seat* can be left empty and children can offer randomly the character's responses to questions. Further discussion is possible when conflicting answers are offered, with the teacher asking individuals to say why they believe that the character would answer in that way.

This approach encourages children to listen carefully as they need to build their questions onto what has already been said. Also, they hear the teacher and other children framing effective questions and this helps them to develop their own. Teaching children to listen permeates the National Curriculum for English with children's ability to pay attention being a central feature of the shared and group elements of the Literacy Hour.

Mantle of the expert

In the simplest form of this technique, pioneered by Dorothy Heathcote[6], the children take on the role of experts whose knowledge and experience are greater than those of the *teacher in role*. When children wear the mantle of the expert, the roles of teacher and child are temporarily reversed. The child is the 'one in the know', who has the expertise, understanding and experience, with the teacher being the 'one who needs to know', seeking clarification, advice and help. While all in this process are aware that they are simply acting, this reversal of status adds a fruitful new teaching and learning strategy to the repertoire.

When tied into a topic which the children have been studying, an opportunity is provided for the use of subject-specific knowledge and language and for the teacher to assess the levels of understanding achieved. For example, a Year 4 class had been studying the Vikings. When the children entered the classroom for their drama lesson the desks had been pushed back, chairs had been placed in a circle and on a table in the middle was a small collection of dusty looking objects. The children sat down in the circle. The *teacher in role* introduced herself as a local historian, who addressed the children as:

> . . . the world's leading experts on Viking settlements. It is a great honour to welcome you to this important meeting. During a preliminary investigation of a site being cleared for building work by a developer, these artefacts have been discovered and we believe that they may suggest the presence of a Viking settlement.

Here, the teacher is using language with which the children might not be familiar. They are being addressed as adults and 'experts'. She is modelling formal language by using Standard English appropriate to the situation, which helps to underline the serious nature of the enquiry. Children in role as experts respond with the language which they believe to be appropriate to the situation. As each offers suggestions and advice, there is confidence and authority in their speech.

The items were passed around carefully and the 'experts' conferred with each other:

Teacher: 'Could you advise us on how to conduct an investigation of the site and what we should be looking for?'

A sense of urgency was added:

Teacher: 'We only have a week. Builders will begin work on the site after that.'

The children began to talk to each other, still in role.

Maria: 'The builders will have to stop work.'
Jamil: 'They will damage the ruins.'
Teacher: 'How can we stop them?'
Paris: 'We will get the police.'
Jamil: 'I'll phone the Government.'

Out of role, the teacher and children reflected on the learning which had taken place. She drew attention to the language they had used in order to play the parts convincingly. Encouraging constructive criticism, she asked leading questions such as:

'In our drama, what worked well and why?'

Children commented on each others' roles, how what had been spoken and the way it had been said made the drama believable: a metacognitve process implicit in the cycle of making, performing and responding which demonstrates the importance of reflection in drama[7].

Generating text

Drama can provide children with a variety of contexts in which to write for a range of purposes and audience. It is a vehicle both for demonstrating and extending understanding.

Writing in role

Taking the Viking stimulus further, an emphasis was placed on the investigation running out of time, so a campaign was launched to halt the building work for a while. The children looked at a variety of newspaper articles and then produced their own about the archaeological investigation in styles appropriate to a particular type of media. There were 'sensational' reports for the tabloids, exploiting the children's knowledge and use of alliteration. Thirty-second scripts were written for radio and television coverage, the range and style of writing needing to match with the type of programme. For example, some 'reporters' attempted to write serious, factual accounts of the campaign for the BBC nine o'clock *News and Weather*, others for Channel 4's *The Big Breakfast* news slot, whose coverage features sensational language similar to that typifying tabloid front page journalism, rich in alliteration and 'catchy' phrases:

Newsreader: Good morning. Hot sounds from under the ground. There's a to-do at Sutton Hoo. The archaeologists are up in arms and down in the dumps about the crafty contractors creeping onto their dig to build homes on some old bones. (Michaela, aged 8)

A group of children wrote a script for a short item on the campaign for the *Blue Peter* programme, tailoring their writing to suit a 'younger' age range with a more limited understanding of archaeological issues. As a result, the children were learning about genre and writing for a variety of audiences.

Scribing

To extend the potential for writing which can be obtained through drama the whole class, *in role*, could write with the teacher acting as scribe. This activity has a number of benefits:

- The teacher models the writing and thereby shows the correct style.
- The teacher and children compose collaboratively.
- As they refine and edit, the children are having to pay close attention to both the composition and transcription elements of the text.
- The teacher can provide differentiation in a number of ways: for example, by targeting specific children with different questions, reading the text aloud with those who lack confidence, and so on.
- Children who might only manage one or two tortured lines unaided are able to contribute to the whole text.
- Most children will feel a sense of achievement from having contributed to the composition of a piece of writing which is of a higher standard of work than would have been possible if they had been working on their own or with a group of peers.

The children of a Year 3 class, as citizens of Hamelin, had sent letters to the local council to complain about the growing rat problem. A 'letter' had come back to them all saying that 'as only a small number of you are affected' the council did not think it to be a serious problem. Children as individuals, groups or the whole class respond very positively to letters written to them within the context of drama. That they should have been sent a reply reflects the 'seriousness' of their endeavour and, assuming they know that it is the teacher who has produced the letter, shows them that their work is respected and taken seriously by her or him.

The 'citizens', with the teacher as scribe, decided to send a communal letter, with a forceful message:

> Dear Mayor,
>   We are ALL very serious about this rat problem, not just a few of us. We're fed up with it. Please will you do something about it?
>   We have to keep our children in the house. They can't go out to play in case the rats get them. How would you like it?
>   Rats spread diseases. If we are ill, we don't go to work. Then who will work for you? No-one!
>   Take a trip to other cities. See how they keep rats out and ask them to tell you how to do it.
>   Don't forget we voted for you. It's your job to look after us. If you don't we won't vote for you again.
>   Clear up our city before it's too late.
> Yours sincerely,
>
> The citizens of Hamelin

Once the children had gone through the process, aided by the teacher, of composing, refining and editing the letter, the teacher wrote it out and brought it back into the classroom for the children to sign, which they did, with pride. Drama had given a sense of purpose to their work and enhanced their understanding of how to write effectively in a persuasive style.

The quality of learning within independent group work is enhanced when children have experienced whole-class teaching such as this, based on teacher modelling, discussion and interaction, maximising their potential for exploratory talk. The guidelines for English in the National Curriculum identify that for group discussion and interaction to be successful, children should:

a) take turns in speaking and listening;
b) relate their contributions to what has gone on before;
c) take different views into account;
d) extend their ideas in the light of the discussion;
e) give reasons for opinions and actions.

(DfEE 1999)

Children of a Year 5 class, in the role of detectives, were investigating the disappearance of a teenage boy. The classroom was set out as normal, with children seated in their groups around tables. This suited the layout of an 'incident room', with groups of detectives working together on the case. After an initial briefing by the coordinator of the investigation (*teacher in role*) the detectives (assuming the *mantle of the expert* [6]) were shown possible clues surrounding the case to date which included a note purportedly written by the boy, a letter he had received the day prior to his disappearance, a train ticket and a brief statement from his mother. Through group discussion, the teams were to come up with a possible scenario and suggestions for ways forward with the investigation, including a plan of action. The activity involved them in both reading and writing in role. Each group had to prepare their findings in the format of a brief report [8] to be fed back to the whole group in the plenary.

Groups of children working in role demonstrated a sense of purpose and clear awareness of each other's function. They listened and argued with the respect appropriate to the 'expert' part they were playing, assessing evidence, responding to the thoughts and opinions of others and taking into account different views while having to justify their own.

Eavesdropping

The teacher interrupted the groups as they worked:

Teacher: 'Remember the point in the discussion you have just reached. Let's listen to each group of experts as they discuss the case.'

She allowed time for groups to recap and then asked for silence. She moved around, pausing for a minute or so by each group, which was the signal for that group to resume their discussion, loud enough for everyone else to hear. When all groups had presented their 'snapshots', she asked questions of everyone, based on what they had just heard:

Teacher: 'Which groups were thinking along the same lines in their theories of what had happened? What were the main areas for disagreement for *this* group?'

The strategy of eavesdropping, accompanied by teacher questioning, is highly focused and constitutes a brief interruption which allows time to observe everyone's work. It brings together work in which the whole class is engaged, in this case, heightening the dramatic tension and purpose of an incident room. It also reinforces the need to listen to each other and gives children the opportunity to hear others engaging in exploratory talk, sometimes working with unfamiliar language. The teacher did not need to monitor the groups closely. This was high quality and largely independent oral work, but they would not have been able to achieve this had they not learned to work in this way with the teacher in previous lessons.

Drama and text

All the strategies described so far can be used to help children interrogate text, such as the use of still image to represent key moments in a chapter, slowing down the narrative, especially with texts which are plot-driven; hot seating characters and role-playing events which contribute to the sub-plot of a story and writing in role.

The empathy/understanding dimension of drama work is inevitably stimulated through texts of one sort or another. Therefore, drama can be used to aid understanding at text level as envisaged in the Literacy Hour. For example, the children in a Year 6 class were reading *The Diary of Anne Frank* as part of a topic on the 1930s. In using drama strategies to explore the text, the intended learning outcomes were that the children would:

- Interrogate a text 'with challenging subject matter that broadens perspectives and extends thinking'[9].
- Gain a perspective about a historical issue.
- Reflect upon their own responses to change.

Like Anne at the start of her diary, the children were approaching puberty. Some were anxious about the transition to secondary school. One girl was a Bosnian refugee who had recently joined the school. The safe context of the story helped the children explore and reflect upon the anxieties they were experiencing about changes taking place in their own lives.

An initial improvisation coincided with the time when the class had reached the part of the diary where Anne describes the family's preparations for going into hiding. The children, working in role and in groups which represented families or flatmates, were asked to make decisions about which of their possessions they would take with them if they were asked to go into hiding. Part way through the improvisations, the teacher interrupted to ask them to imagine that each group had been given a large cardboard box which, due to lack of space,was all they would be allowed to take with them. By these means extra pressure was put on the children to argue, discuss, prioritise and ultimately compromise on their original list.

Some 'families' agreed to scale down what they would take, in terms of size and quantity of objects. Some members had chosen to take a lock of hair, pictures of loved ones, letters and gifts given to them by friends they might never see again. They listened attentively to each other. The atmosphere was one of sustained concentration, mutual respect and a communal sadness at leaving their homes.

This activity, conducted in groups with little or no intervention from the teacher, demonstrates ways in which drama contributes to creating and sustaining purpose for independent group discussion and interaction. In this lesson, group talk featured through taking turns in speaking and listening, taking different views into account with sympathy and understanding, extending ideas in the light of discussion and giving reasons for opinions and actions. Such activities promote oral work which is discursive and interactive, a significant aim of the National Literacy Strategy. The teacher asked the children if this moment had reminded them of any time in their own lives which they were invited to share with the rest of the class. Their responses included moving house, leaving an area, saying goodbye to a grandparent going home to India, coming home from holidays, hiding in a bomb shelter in Kuwait and leaving friends made while away.

While it is possible to plan a drama activity and identify clear learning outcomes, the teacher cannot know what personal response the drama may generate. In this instance, the experience had provided a vehicle for the children to put into words their own emotional response to events which they may never have discussed before. The children were learning to empathise both with characters as well as with each other. At the end of the lesson, the teacher invited the children to reflect upon the quality of the exploratory talk which they had achieved in their groups and the way in which such talk enhanced their learning and understanding; a metacognitive process stimulated by engagement in, and reflection upon, drama.

Some of the drama work on the Anne Frank story had stimulated writing *in role*: diary entries of different characters, letters from hiding, letters sent from the outside *to* those in hiding, giving news of events, some even written in elaborate codes. They all displayed and extended understanding of the issues the children explored through the drama. Of equal importance is reflective writing *out of role*, articulating thoughts and emotions which arise through dramatic engagement with a text, demonstrating empathy and conveying this to an audience. As Naomi, aged 11, commented: 'I think that people who are witnessing a war, losing friends and family and homes can never recover. For this must be like a knife cutting through their lives.'

Reading text aloud

When working with text, children should be encouraged to read aloud, with expression, characterisation and pace, as modelled by the teacher. This approach is of particular significance in the shared reading aspect of the Literacy Hour. In this way most teachers, when reading or telling stories to their classes, incorporate drama to some degree in their delivery, changing their voices with volume, tone and pitch, adopting accents, using facial expression, establishing eye contact with the 'audience', all of which enhance enjoyment and understanding. Children will then develop awareness of how meaning can be both illuminated and altered by the ways in which text is spoken and their listening skills, as well as their understanding, can be developed in this way. Text which was written to be performed should be lifted from the page and heard, encouraging 'attentive listening and response'[10]. But how is a teacher to manage reading aloud a play text written for a small number of speakers, with a class of 30 or more?

With a script written for two characters, the class can be divided into two lines facing each other. Everyone is given a copy of the text. All those in one line play part A and all those in the other, part B. Begin with the first pair and move down the lines as the script progresses. Come back to the first pair and continue until the script is finished. The teacher, or a child, reads stage directions. In this way, everyone will need to concentrate on following the text, to look ahead for their turn, and all of the children will speak. There will be a variety of delivery. When the text has been read through once, with difficult or unusual words being identified and discussed, teachers can ask a range of questions, all of which will require the children to re-examine the text or to reflect on what they have heard. They can ask children to consider directions, pauses and actions which will add or enhance meaning: how, for example, speaking the text with an angry, sad, happy or frightened vocal expression can create a different context and meaning. Again, working in groups, using just a part of the whole text, children could plan and rehearse their own version of it to be performed to the rest of the class.

Understanding a challenging, dramatical text

Classical texts can be used, even with very young children. Shakespeare, for example, is challenging to all, adults and children alike, and of those people going to see a performance of one of Shakepeare's plays, very few will have a thorough understanding of the language used. However, carefully selected short scenes and speeches can provide highly enjoyable dramatic experiences in the classroom. Here are some examples of the ways in which teachers could work with excerpts in the primary school.

The Tempest, Act III, Scene 2: Caliban's speech

Caliban: Be not afear'd: the isle is full of noises. Sounds,
            and sweet airs, that give delight and hurt not.
            Sometimes a thousand twangling instruments will
            hum about mine ears, and sometimes voices,
            that, if I then had waked after long sleep,
            Will make me sleep again: and then, in dreaming,
            The clouds methought would open and show riches
            Ready to drop on me, that, when I waked,
            I cried to dream again.

Activities: 'The Isle is full of Noises' (The Tempest)
Suitable for Key Stages 1 and 2

WHOLE CLASS

- Read through together, aloud.
- Identify difficult words.
- Question children about possible meanings of unusual words and phrases.
- Read through, singing the word which precedes punctuation.
- Read through, kicking up a balloon or scarf at the end of each phrase.

- Allot each child a phrase (each will be spoken by at least two children).
- Place chairs all around the room to represent trees in a forest; each child stands behind a chair and when it is that child's turn to speak their phrase s/he must do so while running from one 'tree' to another.
- Discuss ways in which children may additionally animate their phrase. For example: hopping/ skipping/ singing/ doing a cartwheel and so on. As two speak the phrase at the same time, coordinate how it is to be done.
- Heighten the sense of drama by suggesting that in the trees are monkeys with custard pies. As the speakers leave the shelter of their 'tree' they may have to dodge the custard pies being hurled at them!

Macbeth, Act I, Scene 1: The Three Witches

(adapted)   When shall we three meet again?
            In thunder, lightning, or in rain?
            When the hurly burly's done.
            When the battle's lost and won.
            That will be ere the set of sun.
            Where the place?
            Upon the heath.
            There to meet with Macbeth.
            Fair is foul, and foul is fair:
            Hover through the fog and filthy air.

This is one of the shortest scenes written and it is highly charged because it is the dramatic opening scene and involves the supernatural.

Activities: 'Fair is Foul . . .' (Macbeth)
Suitable for Key Stages 1 and 2

WHOLE CLASS

- Seat the children in a circle.
- Set the scene for the 'blasted heath' by discussing what the place would look like. Possibly there will be trees, bushes, ditches, fog and marsh. What would we hear in this place? Build up the atmosphere by asking the children one at a time, around the circle, to add their sounds to create a *soundscape*. 'Conduct' the soundscape, bringing volume up and down and cueing parts of the circle. Hand over the job of conductor to one of the children.
- Read through the scene together.

GROUP WORK

- Divide the class into small groups. Each group will be given a phrase. Brainstorm different ways the words may be delivered, e.g. whispering, echoing each other, varying pitch and volume, singing and so forth.
- Groups should be given time to rehearse.

WHOLE CLASS

- Go through the scene, each group performing their phrase in turn.
- Discuss 'what worked well and why' and possible refinements.
- Repeat performance.

- Recap on the soundscape.
- Rehearse, performing the text over the soundscape.
- Add refinements, such as deciding when the volume of the soundscape should be raised/lowered.
- Give the final 'performance'.

Macbeth, Act V, Scene 1: Sleepwalking

Lady Macbeth: (adapted)	Yet here's a spot
	Out, damned spot! Out, I say!
	One, two; why then 'tis time to do it.
	Hell is murky.
	Fie, my lord, fie! A soldier and afear'd?
	What need we fear who knows it, when none can call our
	power to account?
	Yet who would have thought the old man to have so
	much blood in him?
	The Thane of Fife had a wife; where is she now?
	What, will these hands ne'er be clean?
	No more o' that, my lord, no more o' that; you mar all with this starting.
	Here's the smell of the blood still.
	All the perfumes of Arabia will not sweeten this little hand.
	Oh, oh, oh!
	Wash your hands, put on your nightgown, look not so pale.
	I tell you again, Banquo's buried; he cannot come out on's grave.
	To bed, to bed; there's knocking at the gate.
	Come, come, come, come, give me your hand.
	What's done cannot be undone.
	To bed, to bed, to bed.

Activities: 'Sleepwalking' (Macbeth)
Suitable for Key Stage 2

WHOLE CLASS

- Cut the text into strips – one line per strip.
- Seat the children in a circle.
- Allot lines randomly around the circle so that each child has one.
- Set the context by reading a description of the sleepwalking scene.
- Choose a child to represent Lady Macbeth.
- Lady Macbeth walks around and across the inside of the circle. Each child that she passes speaks her/his line (sometimes the lines will overlap).
- Discuss 'what worked well and why' in relation to individual delivery, combination of lines, and so on. Refine: 'How can we improve upon the performance of the scene?' Possibly add a *soundscape*.
- Read through again, with added effects.
- Tape record the scene, as if making a radio drama.
- Ask 'Where have we come across these lines before – to which parts of the plot do they refer?'

EXTENSION: Some children may search text of play using a *Macbeth* CD ROM.

GROUP WORK

- Give each group an envelope containing a complete set of lines, cut into strips.
- Ask the groups to attempt to put their lines in the order in which they think they were written.
- Plenary: compare and contrast versions. Look at copies of scene as written, including other characters.
- Compare with an earlier speech of Lady Macbeth's, in verse. Why did Shakespeare choose to write this final speech of Lady Macbeth's in prose?

Conclusion

In the examples of classroom practice which have been discussed in this chapter, it is evident that drama:

- has a unique contribution to make in the teaching of speaking and listening
- has potential for literacy learning
- offers a range of strategies applicable to text level work
- is a vehicle for imaginative response to, and generation of, text
- helps children gain an understanding of the deeper meanings in books
- stimulates enquiry
- builds confidence
- promotes discursive, exploratory talk which is a significant aim of the National Literacy Strategy, particularly in fostering independent group work.

In adopting drama approaches, not only is the teacher enhancing her/his repertoire of teaching strategies, but the children are learning many skills which will contribute to their development as independent learners, and not just in literacy, but across the curriculum. We should all be saying, ' Yesss!' to drama.

Notes

1. Fleming (1994) *Starting Drama Teaching.* London: David Fulton Publishers.
2. C. O'Neill (1995) considers the importance of empathy in the process of drama.
3. *National Literacy Strategy: Framework for Teaching* (DfEE 1998). Year 2, text level work 4, to predict story endings and incidents.
4. The author, cited in J. Bowden and F. Marton (1998), explores children's thinking when generating and shaping drama to convey meaning to an audience.
5. An expression coined by P. Baldwin (1991) to represent the process of negotiating meaning children undergo when creating a 'still image'.
6. D. Heathcote and G. Bolton (1995) explore the 'mantle of the expert' approach.
7. Here the teacher's intervention in role serves to 'scaffold' the children's understanding. See L. Vygotsky in A. Pollard (1997) p. 111.
8. D. Wary and M. Lewis (1997) advocate giving children the opportunity to explore formal and abstract writing through preparing reports.
9. *English in the National Curriculum* KS2 Programme of Sudy, Reading. (DfEE 1999)
10. *English in the National Curriculum,* (DfEE, 1999).

Further reading

Baldwin, P. (1991) *Stimulating Drama – Cross-curricular Approaches to Drama in the Primary School*. Norwich: Norfolk County Council.

Bowden, J. and Marton, F. (1998) *The University of Learning*. London: Kogan Page.

Clipson-Boyles, S. (1998) *Drama in Primary English Teaching*. London: David Fulton Publishers.

DfEE (1998) *The National Literacy Strategy: Framework for Teaching*. London: HMSO.

DfEE (1999) *English in the National Curriculum*. London: HMSO.

Fleming, M. (1994) *Starting Drama Teaching*. London: David Fulton Publishers.

Garfield, L. (1988) *Shakespeare Stories*. London: Heinemann.

Garfield, L. and Foreman, M. (1985) *Shakespeare Stories*. London: Victor Gollancz.

Heathcote, D. and Bolton, G. (1995) *Drama for Learning: An Account of Dorothy Heathcote's 'Mantle of the Expert' Approach to Education*. Portsmouth, NH: Heinemann.

O'Neill, C. (1995) *Drama Worlds*. Portsmouth, NH: Heinemann.

Pollard, A. (1997) *Reflective Teaching in the Primary School*. London: Cassell.

Woolland, B. (1993) *The Teaching of Drama in the Primary School*. Harlow: Longman.

Wray, D. and Lewis, M. (1997) *Extending Literacy: Children Reading and Writing Non-fiction*. London: Routledge.

CD-ROM
BBC (1996) Shakespeare's *Macbeth*. London: BBC Education/Harper Collins.

Chapter 8

'Where am I going?': planning and assessing progress in literacy

Deborah Jones

Assessment helps me know where I'm going. (Robena, aged 10)

Introduction

Assessment and planning are inextricably linked. As Robena has noticed, knowing what we have achieved and how well we have achieved it enables us to plan for the future and to map out the way ahead. This process is at the heart of effective teaching and learning. Planning, teaching, learning and assessing form a cycle with each aspect being bound up with the other, so that they are in a sense interdependent. Planning must be based on what children can actually do, as awareness of their knowledge, skills and understanding is integral to effective further teaching. Language pervades the curriculum, therefore the assessment of literacy is of fundamental importance. Accurate assessment can be a powerful motivator for both teachers and children as they see what has been achieved and are enabled to plan the next learning steps. What is good practice in the assessment of literacy applies to assessment in any aspect of the curriculum. The aim of this chapter is to consider the role of assessment in planning and teaching literacy and to show how the use of a variety of strategies can catapult children forward in their thinking and learning.

Assessment – power and mystique

Assessment is a powerful force as its results are used to categorise individuals. The process starts at a very young age and culminates with the award of various qualifications that can ultimately decide the course of adult lives. For some assessment is viewed positively, for others it is something to be endured or at worst something to be feared. Individual teachers and whole schools are held accountable for the standards they achieve, as is evidenced in published league tables in which assessment has a crucial part to play. Results have been used by both government and media and are often at the centre of disputes about falling standards. The equally hot topic of *poor standards in literacy* has been in the press for a long time. Therefore, mixing literacy and assessment together makes an explosive brew! There seems to be little in common between teachers' views and those of the wider public. Why is this? Could it be that as a profession we have perpetuated a mystique surrounding our knowledge of teaching literacy and our knowledge of assessment? There are many doors to be unlocked concerning the assessment of literacy and the main aim of this chapter is to examine ways of sharing this knowledge with parents and children, so dispelling this mystique in order to create effective partnerships with all concerned in the education of the child.

The purposes of assessment

> I did it because I had to. My records were complete and levels assigned – but I never quite got to grips with using them to help me plan really specifically. (Year 2 teacher)

Here, one teacher describes her experience of assessment. This is where we should start, as examining what we believe will influence our actions. Asking certain questions will be helpful in this: for instance, why are we assessing children? What are the real reasons for this?

Clearly the purposes of assessment are many and varied. They include:

- to record progress
- to diagnose particular difficulties
- to provide feedback for parents
- to inform planning and teaching
- to comply with legal requirements
- to be accountable to outside bodies
- to help children learn
- to gauge how effective teaching has been.

It is a useful exercise to consider the reasons why we as teachers assess children and what the most important motivators are likely to be.

The principles of assessment

In order to guide our thinking and practice in assessing pupil progress the following principles can be identified. Assessment should be continuous, curricular, consultative and communicative. The importance of each of these will be considered in turn.

Assessment should be curricular

Traditional approaches to assessment have been one-shot procedures often bolted on to the curriculum but not integral to it. End of term examinations and isolated tests characterise this approach. The Task Group for Assessment and Testing (TGAT) (1987) stated that assessment should be an integral part of the curriculum and that it needs to take place within a strong context of meaning, as it is crucial that children make connections between what they are doing now and what they need to learn next[1]. If

Assessment should be continuous

If assessment is central to teaching and learning then it must be built into the daily routines of the classroom. It needs to provide both 'feedback' and 'feedforward', showing what children have achieved and how this will enable them to move on. If learning is a continuous process then assessment must be, too. Some traditional approaches have viewed assessment as occasional rather than continuous but this does not fit in with what we know about how children learn. It is essential that they are given several opportunities to show what they can do, as catching them on an off-day will do very little to help them move forward or to inform future teaching.

Assessment should be consultative

Teachers do not have exclusive knowledge of the child. Parents and carers have a wealth of information which can be drawn upon to support teaching and learning. We have all worked with children who exhibit completely different behaviours at home and school and discovering why this is can trigger a whole new range of approaches to teaching. Assessment is not solely the domain of teachers, as other adults, for example volunteer reading helpers (when informed appropriately), can be used to note achievement and gather information. Central to this process, however, are the children themselves. Why should assessment be seen as the exclusive domain of the teacher? Conferencing with children to discover what they know and to elicit reflections on their learning can be a most powerful aspect of assessment[2]. Enabling parents, carers and children to contribute to this process is at the very heart of effective assessment. Cultivating such partnerships needs to be integral to both our practice and our thinking.

Assessment should be communicative

If assessment is not the exclusive domain of the teacher then methods of recording and the ways in which progress is discussed should be accessible to all. Therefore, letting parents and children in on the processes of assessment is vital, including setting up strategies in which all the parties concerned know what is being assessed and why. Results of assessments also need to be transparent, for example through avoiding jargon for non-professional audiences and by taking care to communicate in ways which are meaningful to all. (This will be discussed in more detail later.)

Think back to your own experiences of assessment:

- What are your earliest memories?
- What do you remember about assessment in school?
- What other types of assessment have you experienced outside of a school context?
- What feelings characterise your different experiences?

Apply the four principles of assessment to your own reflections about yourself and to your classroom practice. How do they match up?

Methods of assessing literacy

The four principles above should underpin any form of assessment undertaken in schools and underlie the various methods of assessing literacy discussed below. Several different methods need to be used so that a range of evidence is collected relating to each child's achievements. These could include:

Methods of assessing writing

- National Curriculum criteria, as in the level descriptions
- alternative criteria from other published sources

- Standardised Assessment Tests (SATs) materials
- samples of children's writing
- annotated samples of writing across a range of genres
- developmental checklists
- conferencing and self-assessment.

Methods of assessing reading

- National Curriculum criteria as in the level descriptions
- using the 'Framework of Objectives' of the National Literacy Strategy
- alternative criteria from other published sources
- SATs materials
- reading scheme levels
- miscue analysis/running records
- standardised reading tests
- observation samples
- book reviews
- developmental checklists
- conferencing and self-assessment.

Methods of assessing speaking and listening

- National Curriculum criteria as in the level descriptions
- alternative criteria from other published sources
- observation grids
- developmental checklists
- conferencing and self-assessment.

Examples of these methods are given below.

Using specific criteria is a common way of assessing children. Such criteria may be selected from the *English in the National Curriculum* documentation[3]. Alternatively, the teacher may also identify her/his own criteria for a particular learning activity which the child can be assessed against. Developmental checklists may be used to record progress across each of the Programmes of Study for English[4].

Observation grids or formats are a means of recording what a child is doing during a specific activity and provide evidence of the child's achievements at that time. The example in Figure 8.1 may also be used as a checklist/planner for individuals or groups.

ACTIVITIES	PARTICIPANTS e.g. – pair, individual to group, individual to class	TYPES OF TALK

Figure 8.1: Speaking and listening checklist/planner

Speaking and listening may be assessed within any curriculum area and the following observation grid (Figure 8.2) has been devised for this purpose. While focusing on the chosen child tick off those words around the edge which best describe this speaking and listening behaviour. This may then be written up in prose form in the 'record of

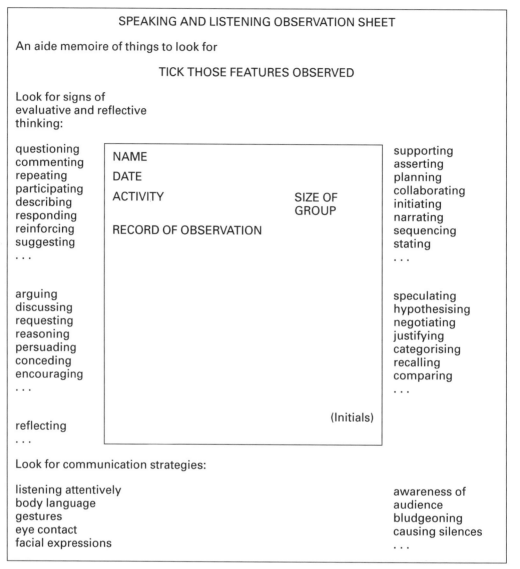

SPEAKING AND LISTENING OBSERVATION SHEET

An aide memoire of things to look for

TICK THOSE FEATURES OBSERVED

Look for signs of
evaluative and reflective
thinking:

questioning
commenting
repeating
participating
describing
responding
reinforcing
suggesting
. . .

NAME

DATE

ACTIVITY   SIZE OF
                                            GROUP

RECORD OF OBSERVATION

supporting
asserting
planning
collaborating
initiating
narrating
sequencing
stating
. . .

arguing
discussing
requesting
reasoning
persuading
conceding
encouraging
. . .

speculating
hypothesising
negotiating
justifying
categorising
recalling
comparing
. . .

reflecting
. . .

(Initials)

Look for communication strategies:

listening attentively
body language
gestures
eye contact
facial expressions

awareness of
audience
bludgeoning
causing silences
. . .

Figure 8.2: Speaking and listening observation sheet[5]

observation' section and becomes evidence for the assessment of speaking and listening.

Collecting a range of samples of children's work to be kept as evidence of achievement is most helpful particularly when annotated so that their significance can be recalled at a later date (see Figure 8.3).

In addition, book reviews may provide useful records of the child's reflective thinking about the content of a book (see Figure 8.4).

Literacy conferences (i.e. conversations about children's perceptions and abilities) with both parents and children may also be used to gather evidence for all aspects of language development.

Miscue analysis is a method by which the teacher analyses the child's miscues when reading a text aloud. This procedure, devised by Goodman[6] in 1973, has been simplified into the form of a running record. These approaches may be used with

Name _____

Year group _____

Subject/Activity _____

Date _____

Activity: Individual   Pair
Group (Please circle)
Degree of Peer group support:
None 1 2 3 4 5 Much
Teacher support: None 1 2 3 4 5 Much

Description of writing
(audience, purpose, type, draft number etc.)

Child's own response to writing

Figure 8.3: Writing context sheet

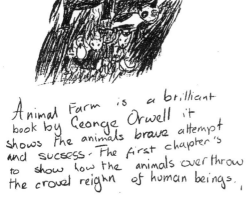

It later shows how the animals later came as tyranical as. the human race,
It shows the croolty of the lead pig Napoleon, is illustrated to the full when a chapter of a brave faithful Horse, Boxer, is taken to the knackers. The ending pargraph shows how the very ten comand- ments made by the animals themselves. are brocken.

Animal Farm is a brilliant book by George Orwell it shows the animals brave attempt and sucsess. The first chapter's to show how the animals over throw the crovel reighn of human beings.

Figure 8.4: Completed book review

young children learning to read or with children experiencing reading difficulties. Useful insights may be gained into how a child decodes print which can inform future teaching in a specific and effective way.

At the end of each Key Stage, teachers are required by law to administer SATs for reading and writing which are used to determine levels of attainment for each child and these are communicated to their parents. For speaking and listening, the level is assessed by teachers alone, so it is important that a range of assessment tools is used to ascertain children's achievement for this particular attainment target.

Teachers need to decide what is to be assessed, how they should do it and when it should be done. At selected points throughout the year all or some of these methods may be slotted in as part of a systematic process. How such a systematic approach can be achieved will be discussed next to show ways in which assessment can be built in to the teaching and learning cycle.

The process

> I've been a teacher for years and I suppose it all comes naturally but when I take time out to really think about what I'm doing, that's when I realise changes are needed for myself and the children to grow. (Year 6 teacher)

How can teachers teach and children learn in an effective way and what part does assessment play in this? After some time in the profession this may become an almost intuitive process, but nevertheless, reflection on practice can give continuing fresh insights[7].

Reflect on the process of teaching, learning and assessing in your classroom.

- What actually happens? Identify the different stages.
- Note down who takes responsibility for these.
- How are the children involved in the various stages identified?
- Compare your list with the one below.
- What are the differences and similarities?

This process may be represented diagrammatically, as in Figure 8.5, to indicate possible stages which may occur in any process of teaching and learning. It can be viewed as a cycle in that setting targets is an integral part of planning itself[8].

The following need to be considered when:

Planning

- selecting/choosing the curriculum content
- planning specific learning intentions for particular lessons, sessions or activities
- planning activities which support the learning of these
- planning assessment of selected learning intentions.

Teaching, learning and assessing

- sharing learning intentions
- fixing learning intentions
- sharing assessment objectives
- fixing assessment objectives
- undertaking activities
- sharing learning
- sharing assessments
- sharing targets
- fixing targets
- recording assessments.

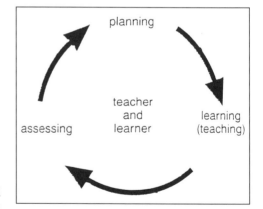

Figure 8.5: Planning, teaching, learning and assessing cycle

These stages are not rigid within the actual teaching situation and they may not always occur in the same order. For example, assessments may be recorded while the children are undertaking the activity as well as at its end. Equally targets may be identified and shared in the middle of an activity as significant learning moments are not restricted to the endpoint. However, there is a sense in which isolating stages and devising formats enables us to deepen our understanding of the teaching situation. Nevertheless, the child must be allowed the freedom to follow individual learning leads within any planned session, difficult though this may be within the constraints of the Literacy Hour.

Planning

One of the most important features of planning is the linking of assessment objectives to the learning intentions by devising them at the same time. It is at the planning stage that assessment needs to be considered, not afterwards. When it becomes an afterthought or is viewed as a totally separate entity, its power as an integral and dynamic part of the teaching/learning process is weakened. A chart on planning formats will help make these issues clear (see Figure 8.6).

Activity Focus	Date
Learning Intentions	Assessment Focus • Who • How • When
Activity Stages • Introduction ——————— ——————— ——————— ———————	Differentiation
Plenary Focus	
Assessment Results	

Figure 8.6: Planning format

Fixing learning

> When I'm starting my work, I need to get it fixed in my head what I'm doing, so then I'll remember it. (Sarah, aged 8)

The notion of 'fixing' is important. Ensuring that children understand what is required of them and fixing it in their memory is crucial. In other words, children, having been told the learning intentions, need to be given a framework or structure to help them remember what they are doing. A written target for example is a way of fixing in the memory a goal to be achieved although this is frequently left out of the process it is critical in securing progress in learning. This process of fixing is one in which children should be given concrete support (see below) to help them make certain aspects of the learning process more explicit. Fixing involves providing aids which enable them to learn about *how* they are learning in the course of developing new knowledge and helping them to make their implicit knowledge explicit through becoming more metacognitively aware. For example, if written targets are locked away in the teacher's mind and not shared with the pupil this 'fixing' will not occur.

What follows are suggestions for developing the different stages of the teaching, learning and assessment process within the classroom context.

Sharing learning intentions

> I always work out exactly what I want them to learn, but I don't always share the detail with them. Perhaps I need to be more specific. (Year 3 teacher)

Learning intentions need to be specific and based on both knowledge of the curriculum and awareness of the children's abilities. Lack of clarity on exactly what children are being expected to learn can result in little learning taking place. Nevertheless, despite clearly formulated plans and sharply focused learning intentions these aims may be of little use if they are not shared with the children, for their aims may be very different from ours. As a consequence, children may only understand a portion of what we want them to achieve and so may only partially succeed in their learning. It is important, therefore, for teachers to make learning intentions comprehensible to children by converting them into a language they can understand. The term 'childspeak' has been coined to describe this process[9]. The teacher may have a distinct focus for learning but this needs to be conveyed clearly to children.

In sharing learning intentions, children need to know about the following:

● *The what*

The activity needs to be clearly explained: for instance, what it is, who it is to be done with, and how long children should spend doing it.

● *The why*

Children should understand what they have to do and why they have to do it. David, aged seven, said: 'I do my work because my teacher says', and this response is typical of what many children think. Helping children to understand real reasons for activities will increase their motivation. They need to be let in on the secret that there is more to a day's work than satisfying their teacher!

● *The audience*

Children should know who will read their writing or listen to them reading or talking. Equally, they need to know what will happen to their work once it is completed. Discussing the options and making decisions with children builds up a climate of trust in which they are free to focus on their work without worry.

● *The genre*

Children need to know whether they are focusing on reading, writing, speaking or listening. If writing, for example, what type or genre are they using, e.g. newspaper report, narrative etc.? Making these aspects explicit is part of the teaching and learning process.

● *The teacher's role*

You, as their teacher, should be clear about what you want from the activity, and what you will be doing to help pupils as they take part in it. Clearly, depending on the task or type of assessment you wish to undertake, your role will vary. Sharing this with children will help eliminate confusion on their part and make it clear what they can expect of you.

In summary, children need to be clear about what work they need to do, its purpose, its audience, and what will happen to it. They need to know both what they should be doing and why, and what the teacher is doing and why. When these issues are clarified through planning formats, such as the one given under 'Planning' (above), the working environment will be appropriately supportive, so that effective learning can take place.

Sharing assessment objectives

> I always tell the children what I'm doing and why. It's important that they know we're all in this together. (Year 2 teacher)

Children need to know *who* will be assessing them. Will it be the teacher, another adult or themselves? In a sense they should be learning a way of working whereby they constantly evaluate their own performance. Ways of achieving this should be built into the daily classroom routines (see below). It is important that children understand what the teacher's role is to be during any session. If you are undertaking specific assessments then they should share this knowledge. What you will be focusing on, why you will be doing it and exactly how. There is no reason why children shoud not see your observation grids or other means of recording. Findings should be shared with them however briefly, either individually, in groups, or at whole-class level within a plenary session. If they understand the process and feel a sense of partnership, then fear, suspicion and awkwardness are removed. The fact that a teacher will be assessing will be viewed by them as a positive and a normal part of a teacher's role.

Providing visual aids and using specific strategies to fix intentions and objectives in children's minds is important. The following list gives examples:

- using a wall chart with stick-on symbols
- asking children to write down one specific intention before they start
- cards with learning intentions on them in the middle of the table
- reminding groups of their learning intentions once they've begun
- setting up a quick memory game/quiz before starting the activity.

Remember learning intentions and assessment objectives can be used for individuals, groups or for the whole class. Figure 8.7 provides a format for this.

The following openers might be helpful to start sessions in order to sharpen the focus on both teaching and learning:

- 'In this session we are going to . . .' (describe the activity itself, who it is to be undertaken with, and how long it will last).
- 'The type of work we are doing is . . .' (describe the type/genre of text).
- 'We are going to do this because . . .' (describe the general aim of the activity).
- 'What I want you to learn is . . .' (identify your specific learning intention).
- 'During the session I will be . . .' (describe your role as teacher).
- 'We will see if we achieve this by . . .' (describe any assessment activity).
- 'What will happen to your work is . . .' (discuss the options for the end result).
- 'At the end of the session we will . . .' (describe the focus of the plenary review).

GROUP 1 ACTIVITY We're going to:	We need to learn:
GROUP 2 ACTIVITY We're going to:	We need to learn:
GROUP 3 ACTIVITY We're going to:	We need to learn:
GROUP 4 ACTIVITY We're going to:	We need to learn:

Figure 8.7: Class wall chart (learning intentions)

Sharing Learning

This may take place with individuals, groups or with the whole class. A useful way of sharing learning is within a plenary session, for example in the last ten minutes of every lesson, as in the Literacy Hour. Much of a plenary's effectiveness is lost if it is used as a rushed 'show and tell' session or a part which must be bolted onto the end of other seemingly more important activities. Careful planning can transform it into a strong motivator and a time when work can be shared and targets developed.

A plenary session can be used to:

- teach children to be reflective
- teach children to be analytical
- develop speaking and listening skills
- develop confidence in themselves as thinkers and learners
- develop a community of enquiry
- develop a secure learning environment
- consider whether or not learning intentions have been met
- enable children to share assessments of themselves and others.

Crafting the plenary is of enormous importance. The following is a suggested format for leading a plenary session:

1. Remind the class of the learning intentions of the lesson
2. Ask groups or individuals to feed back and share what they have done and learnt
3. Invite the class to question or comment on the work of the group or individual
4. Question or provide teacher feedback to individuals, groups and the whole class, asking for example: 'Have we met our learning intentions?'

Ways of feeding back

Having one group feedback thoroughly will be more effective than trying to get half the class to merely say what they have achieved. It is important to be explicit about the nature of the feedback and what language mode(s) the child is being asked to use. We should model questions and types of talk such as interviewing, we want children to become more confident in and use themselves.

There are several ways in which this can be achieved as outlined below.

Reporting

Structuring the end of an activity using plenary focus cards enables childen to see where they are going and provides a framework and focus for their work. Questions may be written on a card and discussed with children at the start of the activity. They need to know at this stage what is expected of them so that they can structure their work accordingly. Questions they might ask include:

- What have I/we done?
- What have we learned?
- What do we need to learn next?

This provides a baseline format but may of course be extended according to the age and ability of the children or, indeed, the nature of the activity itself. The following questions illustrate how reflection may be further developed.

- What did we enjoy most?
- What were we good at?
- What did we have trouble with?
- Who did what?
- Did we work well together?
- If we were doing it again what would we change?
- Did we meet our targets and how do we know this?

Interviewing

One child should be given a selected question(s) to ask another individual, pair or group.

Persuading

The plenary may be set up so that the child or children must persuade the rest of the class that this was a useful and interesting activity.

Instructing

Children may give others in the class instructions, based on their own experience of the activity, in order to let them know how to go about it when it is their turn.

Debating

Two children may debate certain aspects of the task taking opposing points of view.

Describing still images/objects

Children may be asked to present a still image representing a significant moment in the activity and then one or two of them describe it to the rest of the class. (For more on still images see Chapter 7.)

Setting post-activity targets

Purposes

Targets spring from reviewing and reflecting upon work achieved and this is one of the most critical points in the process. Discussing possible targets is at the centre of the learning process. Setting targets consolidates and moves understanding forward, with the target conference providing an essential link between what has been learned and what the child still needs to know. As part of this process children realise what they have learned and are enabled to become explicit about it. By these means they become more metacognitively aware as they come to understand their strengths and appreciate which areas need further development[10].

Teachers have traditionally been the target setters but children also need to learn how to review their own performance and to set themselves meaningful targets. They are more likely to pursue them if they have been involved in their selection. Within the process of target setting a balance should be maintained between recognising achievement and focusing on points for further development. The teacher's input will be crucial in enabling pupils to do this. As children become more familiar with the process, they will be able to take on more responsibility and will learn to set their own targets with increasing relevance.

In setting targets there are a variety of issues to consider, for example whether:

- targets should be set by the teacher, the teacher and child, or by the child alone
- targets should be set with the whole class, groups or individuals
- targets should be set for each of the Programmes of Study for reading, writing, speaking and listening
- targets should be set for literacy in general.   ,

Children need to become used to working in this way and a variety of mechanisms can be used to support them. Some of the targets will be facilitated through talk whereas others may be written down.

Fixing targets

Targets may be fixed in the child's memory in a variety of ways, for example by using cards, sheets, folders or wallcharts. Reflective journals may also be used as a means of clarifying what the targets should be and could be in the form of a blank diary to be filled in by pupils. When learning how to use them children could keep a series of key questions in the front of the journal to help them structure their writing. These could be similar to those suggested for the plenary focus cards.

Target books are another much sharper and more focused form of target setting. The two formats shown in Figures 8.8a and b have been found to be accessible to children and may be adapted according to age and ability.

The first (Figure 8.8a) is one that may be used by young children and requires only a simple form of evaluation and review. The second (Figure 8.8b) is more advanced with the children being required to ask themselves three basic questions, which are:

- 'What have I done well?' (in order to encourage and focus on achievement)
- 'How do I know this?' (in order to show the importance of specific evidence)
- 'What do I need to work on?' (in order to focus on an area for development, thereby setting the new target).

Targets may be written in terms of general literacy or may be divided into reading, writing, speaking and listening. Target books may be filled in whenever a child has

I am good at:	I am going to work on:

Figure 8.8a: Literacy targets: Key Stages 1 and 2

READING DATE What do I need to work on?	How well have I done? DATE What have I done well? How do I know?
WRITING DATE What do I need to work on?	How well have I done? DATE What have I done well? How do I know?
SPEAKING/LISTENING DATE What do I need to work on?	How well have I done? DATE What have I done well? How do I know?

Figure 8.8b: Literacy targets: Key Stage 2: review

completed an activity related to the target, or may be systematically reviewed on a weekly basis. Clearly the nature of targets may vary with some being long-term and some being short-term. The point, however, is that they should be relevant and appropriate to the child. The main aim of target setting, then, is to help bring children face to face with their own knowledge, skills and understanding, to enable them to be metacognitively aware of their own learning, and as a result to be in control of it.

The National Literacy Strategy

The specific methods for assessing literacy discussed earlier need to be used to inform planning of the Literacy Hour, as children will need to be placed in groups of similar ability during the focus guided work time. Planning should be clear and specific in order to make the most of the limited time available.

Although assessment did not feature in the initial National Literacy Strategy materials, recent documentation stresses the importance of setting targets for literacy[11]. Detailed assessment may be undertaken most easily during group guided work time, but there are also opportunities within shared whole-class work, or at the plenary stage, as has been indicated.

Conclusion

Carrying out effective and systematic assessment provides teachers with an exciting challenge. Through it we can find out what children need to know, which in turn helps us plan for their learning more appropriately. Therefore, it is essential that secure and workable frameworks are in place to support the planning, teaching and assessment of learning. These frameworks are crucial for recording progress in literacy in a rigorous way. Children need to be partners in the process and to be given tools which enable them to gain understanding and control over their own learning. As Robena, aged ten, said after reviewing her work in a Literacy Hour:

> Talking about what I planned to write and putting it on my focus card has helped to fix in my mind what I had to do in my writing. Now I know what I've done well, I know what I need to do next time.

Notes

1. The Task Group for Assessment and Testing (TGAT) Report (1987) emphasises the importance of formative assessment.
2. For more on conferencing see J. Graham and A. Kelly (1997) *Reading Under Control* (David Fulton Publishers), in their chapter on 'monitoring and assessing' reading and the 'Primary Language Record'.
3. Criteria for assessment may be found as level descriptions within the *English in the National Curriculum* (DfEE 1995a).
4. For example, the developmental continua included in the *First Steps* (Raison 1996) and published by Longman.
5. From *The Richmond English Record* (1989) as published by Richmond (Surrey) Education Authority.
6. Further information on miscue analysis may be derived from Y. Goodman and C. Burke (1973) *Reading Miscue Inventory* (Macmillan, New York). A. Browne (1998) gives a comprehensive explanation and examples of miscue analysis in practice.
7. A. Pollard (1997) highlights the importance of reflective practice within the primary school context.
8. V. Koshy and C. Mitchell (1993) usefully describe the place of assessment within a cycle of teaching and learning.
9. S. Clarke (1998) underscores the importance of sharing specific learning intentions with children in a language which is accessible to them.
10. The role of metacognition in children's learning is explored by R. Fisher (1998).
11. The importance of setting targets for literacy has been endorsed within the National Literacy Strategy documentation (DfEE 1998).

Further reading

Barrs, M. *et al.* (1988) *The Primary Language.* London: Record, CLPE.

Browne, A. (1998) *Teaching Reading in the Early Years.* London: Paul Chapman.

Clarke, S. (1998) *Targeting Assessment in the Primary Classroom.* London: Hodder & Stoughton.

DfEE (1998) *National Literacy Strategy: Framework for Teaching.* London: HMSO.

DFEE (1999) *English in the National Curriculum.* London: HMSO.

Fisher, R. (1998) 'Thinking about thinking: developing metacognition in children', *Early Child Development and Care*, **141**, 1–13.

Goodman, Y. and Burke, C. (1973) *Reading Miscue Inventory.* New York: Macmillan.

Graham, J. and Kelly, A. (1997) *Reading Under Control.* London: David Fulton Publishers.

Koshy, V. and Mitchell C. (1993) *Effective Assessment.* London: Hodder & Stoughton.

London Borough of Richmond (1989) *The Richmond English Record.* Richmond, Surrey: Richmond Education Authority.

Pollard, A. (1997) *Reflective Teaching in the Primary School.* London: Cassell.

QCA (1999) *Target Setting and Assessment in the National Literacy Strategy.* London: QCA.

Raison, G. (1996) *First Steps.* Harlow: Longman.

Raison, G. *et al.* (1996) *Writing Development Continuum.* Harlow: Longman.

Task Group for Assessment and Testing (1987) *National Curriculum Report.* London: DES.

Chapter 9
'Incredibly Creative Tools': using ICT and multimedia

John Garvey

As a group of 11-year-old pupils were trying to reconstruct a non-fiction passage on screen using the computer program 'Sherlock', in which the challenge was to predict the content of a passage from punctuation, grammar and semantic cues, the following interaction occurred:

Sue: It's 'Stephen started to cross the road to see what he could . . .'
Teacher: If it is this, what might happen next?
Gareth: He might get run over.
Teacher: Can we say what it's all about?
Sue: It's about a boy.
Nicola: He's 18.
Sue: It's about road rage – someone's saying something. Look, there's speech marks.
Nicola: Someone could be yelling something, to warn him.
Sue: Yelling at someone driving a car?

After the activity Sue was heard to comment further: 'When I work with my friends on this it helps me to talk about what I already know about reading.'

The comments above demonstrate some of the potential of the computer in helping pupils to share their own thinking and understanding about the structure of language, or to put it another way, engage in a intuitive but informed 'metalinguistic dialogue' about their understanding of the rules of grammar and punctuation and the way in which these might be used to derive meaning from texts. It reflects a key aspect of the National Literacy Strategy Termly Objectives in relation to pupils developing an understanding of the way in which language is organised at sentence level:

> to use awareness of grammar to decipher new or unfamiliar words, e.g. to predict from the text, read on, leave a gap and return: to use these strategies in conjunction with knowledge of phonemes, word recognition, graphic knowledge and context when reading.[1]

The use of this software demonstrates how Information and Communication Technology (ICT) can be used to develop skills which contribute to the development of the 'literate pupil'[2]. The Government's recognition of the need to develop a literate population equipped to deal with the challenge of the 'Information Age' is complemented by a strong belief in the power of ICT as a tool for teaching and learning. This has been enshrined in the Department for Education and Employment requirement[3] that trainee teachers use ICT in the teaching of the core subjects as a prerequisite for gaining Qualified Teacher Status. In addition, an investment of £930 million is being made in educational hardware, software and ICT training, with the expectation that by the year 2002 all schools will be connected to the Internet and that primary teachers make informed judgements about the appropriate use of ICT in the teaching of English, science and mathematics.

The challenge facing teachers is how best to use the computer to develop those aspects of literacy which are seen to be essential elements contributing to the development of the literate pupil, namely the key skills of reading, writing, speaking and listening. Although in practice these skills are inextricably linked, it is possible to identify ways in which the computer can be used to teach each of these more specifically.

How can ICT develop reading skills?

Talking Books

Both the National Literacy Strategy and the National Curriculum for English stress that pupils should become effective readers by learning to use a range of strategies to derive meaning from texts. There is evidence that talking books (computer-based stories presented on screen through a combination of text, speech and animation) can provide a valuable resource for teachers in reading instruction.

When talking books first appeared on the market in the early 1990s they generated a great deal of enthusiasm and interest from teachers who recognised a novel and original use of the computer with the potential to interest pupils in the process of reading. However, this enthusiasm was quickly tempered by a more sceptical stance regarding the value of talking books as a stimulus for pupils to read traditional printed texts, best summarised by Burrell and Trushell's derogatory description of electronic books as *'interactive eye candy'*[4].

This stimulated a variety of small scale research projects such as those of Medwell which suggested that electronic talking stories can help Key Stage 1 pupils to read traditional printed texts when used as a complement to those strategies normally employed by the teacher in the teaching of reading[5]. She found that sessions where small groups of pupils used talking books displayed many of the positive characteristics of teacher/child shared reading sessions, including enjoyment of stories, talking about characters, identifying with events and making predictions – all essential elements of the process of learning to read. The greatest benefits accrued when the teacher used a combined strategy of hearing pupils read in the traditional manner and allowing small groups to interact with talking books. The current state of research[6] indicates that talking books have potential in:

- helping pupils gain meaning from texts
- teaching elements such as word recognition and phonemic awareness in an enjoyable and lively context
- providing independent access to enjoyment of words for non-readers
- teaching pupils about features of text (e.g. the role of spaces and pauses, which can be highlighted on screen and related to the role of punctuation in clarifying meaning)
- promoting reading as an active rather than a passive process
- generating a positive attitude towards traditional reading materials, particularly in relation to boys and reluctant readers
- providing opportunities for peer tutoring

- developing an understanding of the link between speech and written text
- facilitating group discussion away from the computer and in particular during review sessions within the Literacy Hour.

It should be noted that only limited research has been carried out into the efficacy of talking books as a vehicle for promoting reading of traditional texts. However, the early indications are that this resource can be a useful complement to the range of teaching strategies that might be employed within Literacy Hour reading sessions.

Talking books now have a powerful ally in terms of making the links between writing and speech explicit, in the form of speech recognition software which allows children to compose their own texts and hear them read back to them. This is the 'ultimate phonic resource' (O'Duil)[7] with the power to tell children just how close the link is between printed words and speech, with consequent benefits for children at word and sentence level. He records some evidence of the particular value of the talking word processor for motivating pupils with special educational needs.

Text manipulation software

The use of ICT is subject to the vagaries of fashion, which are often driven by commercial interests. Currently, there is a great deal of interest in the use of the Internet, e-mail and multimedia. While enthusiasm for new technologies is to be applauded, it is salutary on occasion to review practices and software that have been found to be useful in the past. One example of ICT which has seemed to fall from favour is that of text manipulation software. This genre enjoyed a brief period of popularity in the mid 1980s in the guise of 'Developing Tray', written by Bob Moy, and has recently been revived in the form of 'Sherlock – the Text Detective'. The concept behind the software is remarkably simple. Initially, the teacher types in a text, which the computer presents as a blank screen with only punctuation and dashes to show the placing of letters. Pupils are then invited to reconstruct the text through 'buying' individual letters which then appear on screen and from this predict the meaning of words in context. For example, in work involving the use of 'Sherlock', Year 6 pupils had been studying the murder of Stephen Lawrence through a text derived from the 'Newswise' Web site and had contemporary newspaper accounts surrounding the tragedy. In a large group session on the computer they began with a traditional strategy of 'buying' all the instances of the common vowels 'e', 'i' and 'a' and the consonants 's', 't' and 'h'.

This led to a pupil seeing a pattern emerging that indicated that the name 'Stephen' might be in the text, leading to the prediction that a letter 'p' would appear between 'e' and 'h' (Figure 9.1) This prediction showed the pupil's knowledge of the phoneme pattern 'ph' inside the name Stephen. From this the pupils predicted that the surname

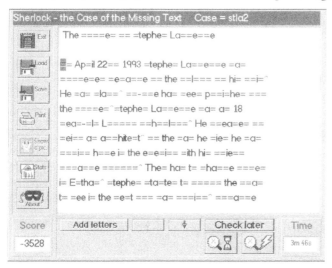

Figure 9.1: Sherlock – the Case of the Missing Text

was 'Lawrence,' that the date was April 22 and the place name (indicated by a capital letter in the second to last line) was 'Eltham'. Thus semantic cues were used, derived from the pupils' knowledge of the events leading up to the murder.

Through a process of discussion, guesswork, inference, prediction and hypothesis – testing based upon their own knowledge of how texts are written or presented – pupils can reconstruct the text on screen through the context of an absorbing 'game', which is motivating and satisfying, drawing upon some of the addictive power of computer software in a positive manner. Govier has commented perceptively that 'the simplest software can foster the most sophisticated thinking'[8]. Despite the simplicity of text manipulation software it has the capacity to develop a wide range of skills which are key characteristics of the literate pupil as defined by the National Literacy Strategy, namely to:

• be able to orchestrate a full range of reading cues (phonic, graphic, syntactic, contextual) to monitor their reading and correct their own mistakes
• understand the sound and spelling system and use this to read and spell accurately
• have an interest in words and their meanings and a growing vocabulary
• understand a range of non-fiction texts
• have a suitable technical vocabulary through which to understand and discuss their reading and writing
• be interested in books, read with enjoyment and evaluate and justify their preferences
• through reading and writing, develop their powers of imagination, inventiveness and critical awareness.

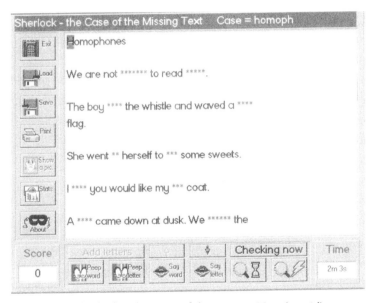

Figure 9.2: Sherlock – the Case of the Missing Text (cont'd)

The versatility of text manipulation software means that it can also be tailored to pupils developing an understanding of very specific aspects of elements of grammar, such as homophones (see Figure 9.2). Text revelations tend to work best with groups of up to eight in a 'community of enquiry' in which pupils can discuss how texts are structured at word, sentence and text level. Teacher questioning is critical in extending pupils' development of skills of inference, prediction and hypothesis-testing.

Reading non-fiction texts: CD-ROM encyclopaedias and the Internet

The unparalleled recent growth of the use of the computer as a resource for accessing information through multimedia CD-ROMs and the Internet provides a particular challenge for the primary teacher.

Despite Anthony Burgess' caustic observation that: 'The transference of the Oxford English Dictionary to a metallic beer mat is one of the major technological achievements of this century'[9], CD-ROM encyclopaedias represent a widely available and accessible media for pupils to explore the world around them. They are now inexpensive (respectable and well designed versions are frequently given away on the cover of computer magazines) and allow access to a wide range of information in a variety of media including text, video and sound. What would traditionally have been stored in a full set of encyclopaedia volumes can now be stored on a single compact disc.

The recent growth of the Internet has been remarkable and fully understandable when we reflect upon the ease of access which it gives to an almost unlimited range of information. A particular benefit for pupils is the opportunity afforded to communicate with experts in their field with a reasonable expectation of an informed reply. One great advantage of the Internet – that anyone can publish their own material – is also its major drawback in that pupils can gain access to offensive material very easily. Additionally, most Web sites are not subjected to an external editing process, unlike written texts or broadcast media. As a result much of what is available can only be described as dross. One strategy that teachers should consider is to encourage the 'bookmarking' of useful Web sites to build up a library of regularly used information to prevent pupils 'surfing' in a time-consuming and wasteful manner.

The growth of the Internet and availability of multimedia CD-ROMs has highlighted the need for pupils to interact effectively with non-fiction texts. This challenge has been recognised for many years with regard to the effective reading of non-fiction texts. Wray and Lewis[10] have commented that:

> Concern about this area is not, of course, new. In their 1978 survey of primary schools . . . HMI found little evidence that more advanced skills were being taught . . . Their 1990 report on the teaching of reading in primary schools makes almost the identical statement.

In using non-fiction resources it is critical that pupils should be clear about what they are trying to find out and have a range of strategies for understanding, evaluating and presenting information. The work of the University of Exeter EXEL project[10] has shed light on the strategies needed to become effective in interacting with non-fiction, resulting in the EXIT (Extending Interactions with Texts) model:

Process stages	Questions
Activation of previous knowledge.	What do I already know about this subject?
Establishing purposes.	What do I need to find out and what will I do with the information?
Locating information.	Where and how will I get this information?
Adopting an appropriate strategy.	How should I use this source of information to get what I need?
Interacting with text.	What can I do to help me understand this better?
Monitoring understanding.	What can I do if there are parts I do not understand?
Making a record.	What should I make a note of from this information?
Evaluating information.	Which items of information should I believe and which should I keep an open mind about?
Assisting memory.	How can I help myself remember the important parts?
Communicating information.	How should I let other people know about this?

In relation to the skills of the EXIT model, the following strategies have proved to be beneficial:

Activation of previous knowledge: the teacher can use a word processor to produce KWL grids. A KWL grid is a frame which allows pupils to record what they already *Know* about a subject, what they *Wish to* find out, how they will find it out and what they have *Learned* from the process. The pupil can use a word processor to brainstorm and record ideas – key ideas can be highlighted, presented in tabular form and edited for future reference.

Establishing purpose: pupils can use the word processor to brainstorm, draft and edit key questions concerning what they wish to find out. Such work can inform the generation of KWL grids.

Locating information: pupils can be encouraged to research a range of resources including traditional printed texts. If they are accessing information using CD-ROM encyclopaedias they need to be taught specific search strategies. These tend to rely on an understanding of a few specific terms which help to pinpoint articles immediately relevant to the enquiry. The following search terms or 'operators' are used by most CD-ROM encyclopaedias:

Operator	Function
'pride and prejudice'	finds every article in which the phrase – 'pride and prejudice' appears (note the use of inverted commas)
pride AND prejudice	finds every article in which both words – pride and prejudice – appear
pride OR prejudice	finds every article in which either the word pride or the word prejudice appears
pride NOT prejudice	finds every article in which the word pride but not the word prejudice appears
pride NEAR prejudice	finds every article in which the word pride appears within eight words of the word prejudice

Such search terms also apply to the use of search engines on the Internet. A search engine allows the pupils to find specific Web sites which might relate to their enquiries. Some useful search engines for pupils are:

Yahooligans (www.yahooligans.com) – a simple and safe search engine for pupils from 8 to 14
Ask Jeeves (www.ajkids.com) – allows pupils to ask 'natural' questions
KidsClick (http://sunsite.berkely.edu/KidsClick!) – a database of thousands of sites compiled by librarians
Searchopolis (www.searchoplis.com) – filters out objectionable content
Awesome Library (www.awesomelibrary.org) – a database of 12,000 carefully reviewed resources
StudyWEB (www.studyweb.com) – search a collection of 100,000 education-related sites

Adopting an appropriate strategy: pupils can be encouraged to cut and paste passages from CD-ROMs or the Internet into a word processor. This allows the copying of hard text with a view to skimming, scanning and intensive reading. The word processor can be used as device for on screen work using cut, paste and highlighting functions. This can be complemented by off screen work on hard copy with groups of pupils, under sensitive guidance from their teacher, working on editing the writing of peers. A good strategy here is to ensure a positive constructive critique of work through the teacher posing the question, 'Can we say two things we like about this work and give one suggestion to improve it?' Comparisons can be made between on screen and hard copy editing of work.

Interaction with text: text manipulation software such as 'Developing Tray' or 'Sherlock' (as evaluated above) can be particularly powerful in constructing meaning from texts. In addition to this the teacher can use a word processor to alter the sequence of passages of text derived from CD-ROM encyclopaedias or the Internet and challenge pupils to re-order and make sense of it. Teachers can model the highlighting of key words in texts through the use of a word processor and then invite children to develop their own expertise in this area.

Making a record: the teacher can develop writing frames to scaffold pupils' writing in a range of genres. This is explored in more depth below.

Evaluating information: one useful initial strategy is to evaluate newspapers with regard to recognising bias in printed material. Pupils can be encouraged to compare how tabloid and broadsheet papers approach the same news stories and be invited to compose their own versions of the same stories from differing points of view: an example of this is presented in the section on developing writing.

Communicating information: pupils can use word processing and desktop publishing software to draft and edit work with a view to publishing texts in a variety of genres such as leaflets, posters or newspapers. The computer can be valuable in terms of making books for sharing with peers or perhaps to read to younger members of the school community. There is also considerable scope for multimedia authoring: this will be explored in the section on developing writing skills.

How can ICT develop writing skills?

The main ICT tools for developing writing skills are word processors and desktop publishing software. The Nobel Prize winning author Gabriel Garcia Márquez has given testimony to the liberating power of the word processor, claiming that writing had become much easier 'since I made the greatest discovery of my life: the wordprocessor'. From an average of writing one page a day, 'now I can do 20, 30 even 40 pages a day. If I'd had this machine 20 years ago, I'd have published two to three times as many books'[11]. It would be folly to ignore the educational potential of such a tool, particularly with regard to promoting writing of quality from children.

   In the early years pupils can learn quickly that they can produce marks on the screen by typing on keyboards or using overlay keyboards. This can be refined rapidly by asking them to talk about aspects of their own experience with an adult (e.g. a parent) who can act as a scribe on the word processor. The contributions of the whole class can be compiled to make a book to be placed in the book corner or library for other pupils to read, or to be used as a shared text within the Literacy Hour. This is one of the major benefits of using the word processor – multiple copies of work can be produced and shared with others, be it family, friends or people who are unknown to the child. The personal can be made public (with the pupil's consent) through the publication and display of word processed posters, stories, reports or books. Pupils can quickly realise that the sharing of written work is pleasurable, thus promoting the move to composing their own writing on the computer. Short pieces such as poems, menus, jokes, invitations, labels or greetings cards can be an ideal context for small group work for children who have not yet got to grips with using the keyboard quickly and accurately and who thus might struggle with writing longer pieces. Such work can also help pupils to begin to understand that writing serves a purpose, which will influence content, style and presentation.

Pupils as young as six or seven can be taught to redraft their own work[12], which is the major reason for using a word processor. Thus pupils can overcome the obstacle of the third of the *'three R's – 'Reading, wRiting and Rubbing out'* and gain an understanding of writing as a process rather than a rush towards an end product.

As children become more proficient in their writing, keyboard skills and understanding of genre, they can be challenged to write for a specific purpose and audience. For example try producing Tudor newspapers after having considered the contrasting styles and intended audience of broadsheet and tabloid newspapers.

The computer enables the publication of work and helps give writing a sense of credibility. As Lauren, one of the pupils, was heard to comment, 'Now it's on the wall looking like a newspaper you feel more like real writer.' An awareness of audience is critical in promoting writing of quality. Work of this nature can be given authenticity by a preliminary visit to a local newspaper office. One interesting feature that has been observed has been the intense motivational effect of pupils working to a deadline for the publication of their newspapers[13]. The value of such work at text level is made explicit in the National Literacy Strategy Termly Objectives for Year 4 Term 1:

Writing Composition

to write newspaper style reports, e.g. about school events, or an incident from a story, including:

- composing headlines
- using IT to draft and lay out reports
- editing stories to fit a particular space
- organising writing into paragraphs.

(DfEE 1998)

The level of challenge is important as children may be routinely using software at home which is far more sophisticated than that which is available at school. As a case in point, desktop publishing software such as 'Microsoft Publisher' has become far more user-friendly with the result that functions such as altering size of text to create headlines and insertion of dates or issue numbers are carried out automatically, leaving the writer free to focus on telling his or her own story. Consider the following vivid newspaper report on a school trip work produced by a six-year-old boy who had been taught the rudiments of writing text and inserting clip art by his mother. It is interesting to note the memorable incidents of the day as seen through the eyes of Joe (which are perhaps not what the teacher intended!) (see Figure 9.3).

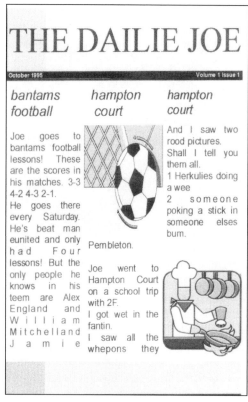

THE DAILIE JOE

October 1995   Volume 1 Issue 1

bantams football

Joe goes to bantams football lessons! These are the scores in his matches. 3-3 4-2 4-3 2-1. He goes there every Saturday. He's beat man eunited and only had Four lessons! But the only people he knows in his teem are Alex England and William Mitchelland Jamie

hampton court

Pembleton.

Joe went to Hampton Court on a school trip with 2F. I got wet in the fantin. I saw all the whepons they

hampton court

And I saw two rood pictures. Shall I tell you them all. 1 Herkulies doing a wee 2 someone poking a stick in someone elses bum.

Figure 9.3: The Dailie Joe

Desktop publishing software is particularly valuable in terms of promoting an understanding of genre in that it employs templates or 'wizards' designed to support the writing of different types of texts, e.g. postcards, newsletters, leaflets, business cards, invitations and greetings cards. This can be profitably combined with CD-ROM software such as Dorling Kindersley's 'The Jolly Postman' which includes templates for children to communicate through letters or e-mail to characters from nursery rhymes and fairy tales.

Writing frames

The National Literacy Strategy requires that children are given the opportunity to read and analyse fiction and non-fiction texts from a range of genres. In order to demonstrate their competence in this area, there is a need for children to record and communicate their understanding. A variety of strategies to support pupils in their endeavours has been proposed earlier in this chapter. The computer can play a valuable role in terms of scaffolding pupils' learning with regard to writing in a range of genres, but can also raise concerns among teachers. A Year 6 teacher was recently overheard commenting at an inservice ICT session: 'I'm not too keen on my kids doing their homework on the computer as all I get back is a three page print out on the Romans or the Vikings or whatever that they've run off from Encarta.'

This phenomenon is not just specific to the use of CD-ROM encyclopaedias. Pupils have been happily copying out reams of text from non-fiction books for many years as proof that they have 'researched' a topic. However, the ease with which electronic texts can be either printed or imported into a word processor poses a temptation that can be hard to resist for pupils who are faced with a blank piece of paper on which to record their thoughts.

The word processor can be a particularly valuable and versatile tool for teachers in this respect as it can be used to produce writing frames[14], which can be tightly focused on the demand of a particular task. Word art and text box functions commonly available on word processors can enable templates to be made, which can structure pupils' attempts at writing for a particular purpose and audience or within a particular genre. This is particularly valuable for work at text level. The writing frame Figure 9.4a and b was produced to support a discussion on the merits of tourism. It is notable how the Year 6 pupil has used the frame to produce a concise and persuasive argument:

There is a lot of discussion about whether tourism is beneficial or not.

The people who think it does help, for example shopkeepers claim that it makes money that can go towards various things in places. They also argue that the tourists can recommend the town to other people and get more people to go to the town/city. A further point they make is about 1 in 20 tourists decide to live in the place they first go to. Even though the tourists damage the natural surroundings, this can get more jobs for people and help people make more money.

However, there are strong arguments against this point of view. Others believe that there is air pollution and litter. Another counter argument is that they could spoil the tradition and tempt hotel companies into building hotels in various cities. Furthermore, they can destroy the things that they come to see; this will eventually wear down people's interest and lose citizens.

After looking at these points, I don't think that tourism is beneficial. This is because tourists are becoming more careless than ever and are beginning to damage everything that they see. I think that anyone who does pollute or damage something should get a fine. This does sound harsh but it is the only way that the tourists will learn.

Figure 9.4a: For and against tourism   **Figure 9.4b:** Tourism – good or bad?

Multimedia authoring and Web page design

Multimedia authoring software allows pupils to construct their own computer presentations using a combination of words, video, animation, pictures and sound. It is analogous to children producing their own CD-ROM resource which can be shared with others on the computer and can vary in scale from a simple page on the screen, which includes text and pictures, to a series of linked screens, which can tell the particular 'story' (which can be fiction or non-fiction) that the pupils wish to relate. The process of constructing a multimedia presentation is similar to that of Web page design in that it requires planning of the whole resource in terms of the 'hyperlinks' that guide the user through linked items of information on different pages.

The simplest starting point can be extremely effective – pupils at Key Stage 1 can be encouraged to use a digital camera. The digital photographs can be transferred immediately to the computer and used as a basis for the pupils' writing simple sentences with each page representing an individual pupil's efforts, which can be linked by computer screen 'buttons' which guide the reader on to the next page. Multimedia software such as 'Hyperstudio' can be used to add video clips and sound, which add enormously to the motivational effect of the use of the computer. As pupils move into Key Stage 2 more thought needs to be put into the initial planning of the multimedia presentation. This is best achieved in small groups away from the computer using pencil and paper to decide the content of each page and the mapping out of the links between each page. An accessible tool for planning can be 'Microsoft Powerpoint', a business-orientated tool for designing slide presentations. This is user-friendly enough

Wimbledon FC are the Greatest!

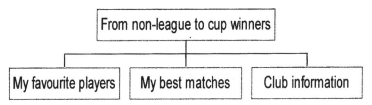

Figure 9.5: Wimbledon FC

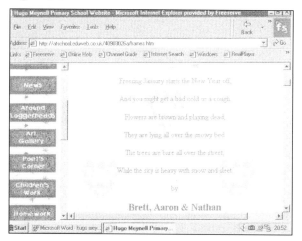

Figure 9.6: Poetry on the Internet

to use with pupils at Key Stage 2, as is evident from the simple plan in Figure 9.5, produced by a group of keen Year 5 football fans.

The same basic planning principles can be used to design Web pages. Most modern word processing software now includes templates to guide pupils through the process of designing Web pages. The screenshot below shows a section of a page from the Hugo Meynell Primary School Web site, demonstrating how pupils' poems can reach a world wide audience (Figure 9.6).

Electronic mail

Part of the appeal of designing Web sites is that electronic mail (e-mail) addresses can be incorporated so that pupils can do more than just publish their work; they can communicate with others around the world immediately. E-mail has tended to be the Cinderella of the ICT revolution, but is of enormous potential in terms of being a motivational resource for writing because of its simplicity, ease of use and potential for rapid feedback. Millum[15] has reported on an exciting shared writing project between primary schools in Sheffield and Scotland which succeeded in motivating boys to write extended collaborative narratives based on the book *Carrie's War*. Such work is particularly interesting in the light of McFarlane's[16] observation that in one primary school experimenting with e-mail, 'boys acted as technicians – happily logging on and downloading namesakes – but it was the girls who engaged with the content and substance of the messages. The boys liked the toys, the girls liked to communicate.'

How can ICT develop speaking and listening skills?

The need for pupils to work together is implicit in much of the work they will do at the computer and in related tasks away from the screen. The computer can provide a powerful arena for children to discuss their own work and that of others, as is clearly evident in some of the work presented above. A further vivid demonstration of this is the way that pupils collaborate out of school on strategies for engaging successfully with computer games. Within school, studies[17] have indicated that there is a strong case for a range of strategies to encourage exploratory talk among pupils at the computer. These range from exercises designed to teach children how to talk together to reach a joint solution to problems, to including the use of key words such as 'because' to justify collective reasons, opinions and ideas. This can lead to an agreed set of ground rules for group talk couched in the pupils' own words, which are rooted in issues pertaining to good quality group talk rather than an over-regard for the need to talk politely.

If the teacher wishes to promote exploratory talk, pupils should be told at the outset that the purpose of the activity is to reach agreed decisions that will be reported back to their peers and/or the teacher. Careful thought needs to be given to grouping pupils:

- The optimum group size tends to be three, except in specific cases such as the use of text manipulation software where larger groups work well in generating a pool of ideas about the text under consideration.
- Friendship groups tend to work well but can fall into the trap of pupils agreeing with each other too readily.
- Gender needs to be carefully considered in terms of pupils dominating the keyboard or taking a passive role.
- At least one of the group should be reasonably able in using the software concerned so as to support others in successfully completing ICT tasks.

It is worthwhile considering software that is not strictly linked to literacy as a vehicle for encouraging speaking and listening skills. Computer control is particularly rich in terms of promoting collaborative problem-solving through the use of programmable robots and the child centred programming language LOGO. Information handling software such as databases and spreadsheets can provide a context for 'cognitive conflict' and decision making with regard to structuring data, searching for information and discussing how the computer is organising information. It is through providing such opportunities for thinking and discussion that the computer becomes a creative tool for learning.

Notes

1. See page 32 of the *National Literacy Strategy* (DfEE 1998) for work at sentence level in Year 3, Term 1.
2. A full description of the 'Literate Pupil' can be found on page 3 of the *National Literacy Strategy*.
3. See DfEE (1998) *Teaching: High Status, High Standards* (HMSO) for a comprehensive description of the capabilities required of student teachers in relation to the use of ICT in teaching the core subjects.
4. C. Burrell and J. Trushell (1997) take a critical stance on the use of talking books in their paper 'Eye candy in interactive books – a wholesome diet?' in the journal *Reading*, July, 3–6.
5. Jane Medwell has carried out extensive research into the value of talking books which is summarised in the following papers: J. Medwell (1995) 'Talking books for teaching reading', *Microscope* **46**, 22–4; J. Medwell (1996) 'Talking books and reading', *Reading* April, 41–46 and J. Medwell (1998) 'The Talking Books Project: some further insights into the use of talking books to develop reading', *Reading*, April, 3–7.
6. For a fuller analysis of research into the value of talking books refer to N. Adam and M. Wild (1997) 'Applying CD-ROM interactive storybooks to learning to read', *Journal of Computer Assisted Learning* **13**, 119–132; M. Chu (1995) 'Reader response to interactive computer books: examining literary responses in non traditional reading sessions', *Reading Research and Instruction* **34**, 352–66 and C. Taylor (1994) 'Teaching reading with talking story books' *Computer Education* **84**, 25–6.
7. P. O'Duil (1994) reflects upon the value of the talking word processor in his paper 'The challenge of the talking word processor', *Microscope* **45**, 3–4.
8. This quote is from an interesting analysis of the information handling skills that can be developed through using the computer, written by Heather Govier (1997) in *Microscope*'s 'Information Handling Special', 2–8.
9. Anthony Burgess (1992). *The Observer*, August 17.

10. This quote is taken from page 1 of D. Wray and M. Lewis (1997) *Extending Literacy: Children Reading and Writing Non-fiction* (Routledge), which also describes the EXIT model of extending reading skills in detail.
11. Cited originally in P. Hamill's (1988) *A Romantic in Cuba* and quotedon page 50 of a comprehensive summary of research into word processing by Ilana Snyder entitled 'Writing with word processors: a research overview', in the journal *Educational Research* **35**, Spring 1993, 49–68.
12. The paper by Kathy Durkin (1997) 'Redrafting at Key Stage 1' in the journal *Reading*, July, 47–50, contains numerous examples of pupils editing and redrafting their work.
13. Refer to D. Wray and J. Medwell (1996) 'Newspapers in education and children's writing' *Reading*, July, 38–43.
14. Refer to M. Lewis, and D. Wray (1997) *Developing Children's Non-Fiction Writing: Working with Writing Frames* (Scholastic) for the rationale for using writing frames and practical ways of using them in the classroom.
15. See Trevor Millum (1998) 'Making the most of email; the virtual writer in residence'. MAPE *Focus on Literacy*, Autumn 1998.
16. P. 170 of A. McFarlane (ed.) (1997) *Information Technology and Authentic Learning* (Routledge).
17. Lyn Dawes and Rupert Wegerif (1998) provide a succinct summary of strategies for enabling speaking and listening at the computer in their paper, 'Encouraging exploratory talk: practical suggestions', which is part of MAPE's *Focus on Literacy Pack*, Autumn 1998.

Further reading

Ager, R. (1998) *Information and Communications Technology in Primary Schools.* London: David Fulton Publishers.
Adam, N. and Wild, M. (1997) 'Applying CD ROM interactive storybooks to learning to read', *Journal of Computer Assisted learning* **13**, 119–132.
Canterbury Christ Church University College (1998) *Talking about Information and Communications Technology in Subject Teaching KS1 and 2.* Canterbury: Canterbury Christ Church University College.
DfEE (1998) *The National Literacy Strategy: Framework for Teaching.* London: HMSO.
Grugeon *et al.* (1998) *Teaching Speaking and Listening in the Primary School.* London: David Fulton Publishers.
Lewis, M. and Wray, D. (1998) *Writing across the Curriculum: Frames to Support Learning.* Reading: University of Reading.
McBride, P. (1998) *The Schools' Guide to the Internet.* London: Heineman.
McFarlane, A. (ed.) (1997) *Information Technology and Authentic Learning.* London: Routledge.
McKeown, S. (ed.) (1994) *Writing and Learning with IT.* London: National Council for Educational Technology.
Medwell, J. (1998) 'The Talking Books Project: some further insights into the use of talking books to develop reading'. *Reading*, May.
National Association for the Teaching of English (1993) *Developing English: Approaches with IT.* Sheffield: NATE.
National Council for Educational Technology (1995) *IT Helps: Using IT to Support Basic Literacy and Numeracy Skills.* London: National Council for Educational Technology.
Wild, M. and Braid, P. (1996) 'Children's talk in co-operative groups', *Journal of Computer Assisted Learning* **12**, 261–71.
Wray, D. and Lewis, M. (1997) *Extending Literacy: Children Reading and Writing Non-fiction.* London: Routledge.

Web sites

BECTA: www.becta.org.uk
English Association: www.le.ac.uk/engsoc
Hugo Meynell Primary School: www.rmplc.co.uk/eduweb/sites/40903026a/index.htm
Literacy Trust: www.literacytrust.org.uk
National Grid for Learning: www.ngfl.gov.uk
Newswise: www.ndirect.co.uk/~sapere/Newswise
Reading Online: www.readingonline.org
Standards Unit DfEE: www.standards.dfee.gov.uk

Chapter 10

'Media and culture': developing literacy for life

Robert Catt and Victoria Whitfield

Often they seemed to prefer the commercial breaks to the programmes themselves.

(Vicky, Year 7 teacher)

Teachers respond to the proliferation of media texts and digital technologies within schools in very different ways. Some welcome what they regard as the promise of excitement and creative challenge; others sense a threat to their existing skills, experience, standards and practice. Differences can become tensions and disagreements when the study of media is included in planning literacy strategies. Our views of media and new communication technologies are bound up with our values and cultural experience.

The initial teacher training experience of the authors provides contrasting experience. One approach – now some years distant – embedded literacy firmly within a reverential respect for the written and printed word. For those trained within this there probably remains a persistent, if implicit, tendency to privilege the book above the film. Yet many more recent trainees are likely to have a broader and more radical view of literacy which includes the ability to use the computer and the video camera and to 'read' the pop lyric and television and film images. When such views impact upon classroom practice it makes for some contentious but productive discussion. For example is the study of soap opera a way of equipping young people with a critical literacy and knowledge which is empowering? Or merely a patronising and second-rate practice which embeds children within a limited cultural context and denies them access to a broader, more demanding range of challenging texts?

This chapter outlines some modest and practical activities relating to media texts. Busy teachers acknowledge the importance of media in children's lives when planning their lessons and when selecting texts, resources and materials. Moving and still images are frequently used as a starting point for discussion or writing. The film of the book (e.g. *Great Expectations, The Borrowers, Gulliver's Travels*) is recognised as a valuable supplement to, rather than a substitute for, reading. Joanna Oldham, for example, describes in a piece of systematic small-scale research[1] the ways in which the use of film enabled 'students to improve their print literacy standards' in studying Dickens's *Oliver Twist*. She illustrates, at least, how 'film can be advantageous in the literacy classroom since it provides a way of gaining access to print texts too dense to be read in lesson time'.

The National Curriculum for English Programme of Study for Reading at Key Stage 2 demands the inclusion of 'challenging subject matter that broadens perspectives and extends thinking' and at Key Stages 3 and 4, texts which 'offer perspectives on society and community and their impact on the lives of individuals' (DfEE 1999). Here the complementary nature of image and word is recognised by many teachers. Joanna Oldham further describes the use of contextual photographs which 'depicted scenes of industrialisation, the workhouse, homeless children . . . in an attempt to convey the poverty of another period'. Such 'images', she suggests 'informed and enhanced the reading of a decontextualised passage concerning Oliver sleeping in the undertaker's workroom. The visual images provided an additional form of access into the text designed to give the students confidence in their ability to make meaning . . .'[1]

Such skilful combination of print and non-print media can provide a powerful teaching resource. It is also potentially demanding in terms of planning time and resource costs. In encouraging teachers to use a wider range of media I will now outline two practical, fairly straightforward and tried and tested activities, which have been used successfully with Year 7 pupils. Each of the activities can, of course, be adapted to include a more sophisticated range of communication technologies. Each relates to advertising within the Year 7 classroom but could also be adapted for use at Key Stage 2 with children from Years 4, 5 or 6.

1. Making a complaint

Media-related literacy activities need not be ambitious. A lively and worthwhile session can, for example, be developed around the design of a 'For Sale' postcard to be displayed in a shop window or on a school noticeboard. There are immediate and productive opportunities for the discussion and illustration of essential information, descriptive language, abbreviations, typography and layout, and the use of ICT. The small scale of the task in itself demands skills of summary and presentation. Discussion can throw up some interesting confusions. 'Why,' asked Darren, 'do they always say "Oh no!"?' It took me a little while to realise that he was referring to 'or nearest offer': Roller Blades, Size 7, almost new, £30 o.n.o.! Discussion is also easily extended to include advertising standards and codes of practice. How honest must an advertisement be? How does the buyer know if the goods are genuine? What are the buyer's rights if things go wrong?

My activity – an oblique introduction to media and literacy – begins with a fictitious mail-order advertisement (see opposite).

Pupils, in small groups, are asked to answer three questions:

1. (Assuming you are interested in the offer) how do you place your order?
2. You wait three weeks but receive no reply. What do you do?
3. After five weeks you receive your tapes. They are badly recorded, out of date 'cover' songs clumsily edited. The boxes are dirty and cracked; your 'free gift' is a creased photograph of a pop star of the 1950s. What do you do?

The questions promote lively discussion: the importance of including a name and address; the need for a parent's cheque or use of a postal order will obviously arise. And so will anecdotes. Children enjoy telling tales of mail-order and catalogue items that have delighted or dismayed the recipients. The question of consumer rights quickly arises. How do dissatisfied customers complain? Are they entitled to a full refund?

Rather than compose letters of complaint themselves, the groups are asked to read and comment on the following example letter:

TOPTAPESTOPTAPESTOPTAPESTOPTAPES

HURRY!! CLOSING DOWN SALE!! HURRY!!

WE HAVE TO DISPOSE OF A STOCK OF
QUALITY SMASH HIT POP TAPES!

RECESSION HIT STOCK BUT QUALITY
GUARANTEED. MONEY BACK OFFER IF
NOT COMPLETELY SATISFIED.

EACH TAPE HAS TWENTY – YES 20! –
CHART-BUSTING SONGS. TOP BANDS!
CHART-TOPPING GROUPS.

BOXED SET OF FOUR DIFFERENT TAPES
ONLY £10 (+ £1.95 P&P)
WE MUST BE MAD!
PLUS FREE SURPRISE GIFT
WITH EVERY ORDER
HURRY! HURRY! HURRY!

CHEQUES/POSTAL ORDERS/CASH
(£11.95) TO
CHARTBUSTERS. P.O. BOX KS O/5
TWICKENHAM. PG CE ENG

Madge Jones,
5 Kathleen Saunders Dwellings,
Twickenham,
Middlesex.

To whom it may concern.
I placed my order for 4 toptape casettes 5 weeks ago. When I wrote you a letter you did'nt even have the curtsey to repley please would you look into this matter for me as I'm worried in case the tapes got lost in the post, I've put my adress at the top of the letter and my phone number is 05050505 and I'm usually in when I get home from school. Thankyou for your trouble and I hope I'm not causing too much inconvinents.
yours truely

Reaction to the letter will range from comments on spelling and punctuation, to layout (why has Madge headed the letter with her name and why has she embedded her telephone number in the text?) and the inappropriate salutation and subscription. More astute observations will point to the way Madge reveals her status (a complaint from a schoolgirl is unlikely to carry much clout) and the conciliatory tone of the final sentence.
    Madge's father now enters the scene with a more dignified formality:

Mr J. Jones
5 Kathleen Saunders Dwellings
Twickenham
Middx
27th/June/00

Dear manager,
    I am writing because youv'e upset my little girl she ordered some pop tapes from you two months ago and shes not heard nothing either you sort yourself out or I'll be round to your place with half a brick.
    I shall give you one week exactly and if I havent heard nothing nor recieved my money back I shall be in touch with my barristers who will sue you for every penny you've got. So you've got seven days or else and I'll go to the enviromental health office too and write to my newspaper.
    I remain respectably yours sincerely,
    Mr John Jones (Madges' dad)

Orthography – layout, spelling and punctuation – will certainly be a continuing focus for comment. There are opportunities here to discuss literacy conventions: not only why letters are constrained by formalities (the placing of addresser and addressee; the appropriate salutation – why do we call someone we may never have met 'dear'? and subscription – why should we be sincere or faithful or true to someone to whom we are making a complaint?). Emerging here, however, should be a sense of the power of writing. Jones senior is unfamiliar with the conventions and this detracts from his credibility. Many pupils will notice, too, how he quickly swings from threat and bluster to anomalous deference. Here there are opportunities to discuss style and tone.

Comparisons are now made with a more conventional and 'correct' letter. This version assumes that the magazine running the advertisement will bear some responsibility for what has taken place and Madge is clearly confident in her awareness of her rights as a consumer.

                                                    5 Kathleen Saunders Dwellings,
                                                    Twickenham,
                                                    Middlesex
                                                    TWI KS05

The Advertising Manager,   27th June 2000
Pop Pickers Weekly,
Gordon House,
London,
EC2 GHT

Dear Sir,
I write to make a serious complaint about 'TopTapes' who advertise in your magazine.

On 21st November 1999, I replied to their advertisement by sending £11.95 for a 'boxed set of four top tapes'. Having received neither tapes nor acknowledgement of my order, I wrote to the company again early in December. I finally received my tapes on 29th December but was outraged to discover that they were badly recorded cover versions of out of date songs. The tape boxes were cracked and dirty and my free gift was a faded and creased photograph of somebody's grandfather!

The 'TopTapes' advertisement is clearly misleading and probably dishonest and I'm sure mine is not the only complaint you will be receiving. I notice that the company has stopped advertising in your magazine and I wonder if they are still trading.

Obviously I want my money refunded in full but I also feel that you should initiate some form of enquiry. I shall also be writing to my local Office of Fair Trading about the matter.

I should be grateful if you could tell me what action you are taking as soon as possible.
Yours faithfully,
Madge Jones

The letter can be offered as a template for pupils' own writing. However, the main purpose of this activity is to involve children in some introductory discussion of media and advertising. The focus here is upon the rights and responsibilities of the consumer and a knowledge of media practice and production. A starting point for an investigation of the persuasive power of the advertiser is an awareness of the rights of the consumer. Follow up activities can include role-play in which a consumer attempts to return a damaged pair of shoes to the manager of a shoe shop who attempts to 'fob her off' with excuses such as: 'sorry, we don't do refunds', 'well, all right I'll send them back to the factory for repair . . .' etc.

2. The world of advertising

Another unit of work is more directly related to media literacy and is planned to provide incremental insight into the world of advertising across a sequence of seven lessons. The teacher refers to the key theme as 'productive response': during each lesson the Year 7 children must produce evidence of their understanding through work of their own; the final lessons will involve the presentation of advertisements designed by groups of children. The following is a summary of the sessions with a comment from the teacher, Vicky Whitfield.

Session 1: Brand name

Children are encouraged to discuss advertisements and their purposes. Does advertising work? If so, how? Children are asked to discuss, in pairs, the impact of advertising upon their own life styles.

Vicky: *I was surprised by the extent to which children enjoyed advertisements, especially those on television. Often they seemed to prefer commercial breaks to the programmes themselves. They particularly liked the speed, compression and humour in advertisements which often seemed to be mini-storied (mini-sagas) with an unexpected punch-line.*

Children are given a list of brand names and are asked to identify the product.

Vicky: *I wanted them to grasp the idea of association and to investigate the likely origins of brand names. Cadbury's, for example, is obviously the name of the manufacturer; there was nothing originally and intrinsically chocolatey about it although the association has been subsequently linked in our minds. But what about Mars? Why is a bar of chocolate named after a planet? And Coca-Cola which probably refers to the ingredients. Could Snickers be a pair of shoes? Could Twix be a washing powder? I tended to concentrate on soft drinks and confectionery and I wanted children to get beyond the taken for granted acceptance of brand names.*

Children are organised into groups and asked to invent a brand name for a new bar of chocolate. Brief presentations are made to the rest of the class with an emphasis on their presenting a rationale for their choice of brand name.

Vicky: *I was surprised how well they responded to the creative thinking involved in inventing a brand name and their presentations gave me a good opportunity to assess their progress in speaking and listening.*

Session 2: Image

Children are given photocopied sheets of advertising images and are asked to discuss the associations, e.g. fun, happiness.

Vicky: *Again, I concentrated on confectionery and I was pushing at the idea of visual literacy – how we 'read' images in particular ways. I used some of the postcard size ads for Maltesers which are given away free in cinemas. The association was always one of fun and the idea of stereotype comes into play: young, 'pretty' models with faultless skin and perfect teeth etc. This was a good lesson for discussion.*

Children are asked to provide an image to support their chocolate product.

Vicky: *Children were familiar with the idea of logo. We did a bit of language history here and I explained that it came from the Greek* logos *meaning word and that a logo is a sign or short version of a word. Children were quick to point out that some ads didn't use words at all: Nike just have a tick symbol (Nike was the Greek goddess of victory, by the way); there's the woolmark and so on.*

Session 3: Slogan and caption

Children are involved in a brief quiz in which products are matched with slogans, e.g. always – Coca-Cola; just do it – Nike . . .

Vicky: *Again, children's knowledge was pretty comprehensive. They easily identified the slogans. We also looked at type-styles and presentations.*

Children are asked to design a slogan or caption for their product.

Vicky: *This time, instead of whole-class presentations, I asked groups to work together, to present their slogans or captions and to provide some positive feedback and criticism.*

Session 4: Target audience

Children, in groups, are given examples of advertisements from magazines and are asked to assign them to the likely target groups.

Vicky: *Here I was trying to get at the idea of the production of advertisements and I talked a bit about market research and the role of the advertising agency. We brainstormed an analysis of a target audience and came up with the categories: age; gender; occupation; domestic status. Age and gender were pretty straightforward but the idea of occupation and domestic status was more complicated. It took some time to get beyond the idea of upper class/lower class. Eventually we grouped occupation into professionals (doctors, lawyers, teachers etc.); managers (supervisors, office workers etc.); skilled workers (electricians, mechanics etc.); other workers (shopworkers, school assistants etc.). In the domestic category we put mothers, fathers, children, teenagers, grandparents, single people.*

Session 5: Campaign

Children are asked to discuss the form and location of advertisements, e.g. television, radio, magazines, posters, etc.
    They are given a schedule from an evening's commercial television coverage and asked to locate ads at appropriate times.

Vicky: *Again, this promoted some informed discussion, e.g. the number of advertisements for toys during morning and evening television for children. We also got into some interesting ethical issues: the animation of toys in advertisements, e.g. dancing dolls; products which couldn't or shouldn't be advertised, e.g. alcohol, cigarettes. Children seemed to have very little knowledge of the costs involved, e.g. peak time television rates.*

Session 6: Preparing presentations

Each group was given a task sheet for the launch of their chocolate bar including brand name etc.

Vicky: *I placed each group in role as an advertising agency. They had to present their campaign with a sketch of the ad and market research support.*

Session 7: Giving presentations

The emphasis in the presentations was on persuasive speaking and listening to an audience. What did they learn from this activity?

Vicky: *They gained an insight into technology and production of advertisements: the role of advertising agencies, and importance of market research seemed new to them. They were involved in some good literacy activities: note-making, presenting ideas etc., some good cross-curricular skills such as problem-solving and groupwork skills and they also learnt at first hand how advertisers seek to persuade an audience.*

Further teaching and learning possibilities include involving pupils in storyboarding for TV, video production, Internet advertisement and desktop publishing.

The rich text of advertising – the interplay of persuasive language and suggestive image – has much potential for the development of literacy skills. In 'reading' and designing advertisements, children have the chance to learn about connotation, the associative resonance of language, in ways which complement their study of poetry and other forms of creative writing. The symbolic power of logos and brand images demand insight and encourage multiple readings. In learning to interrogate these, children learn to interrogate the world. In subjecting the relentless images of commercial advertising to analysis and critical scrutiny they learn to become critical consumers and discerning citizens of the future[2].

If we want our pupils to be active citizens engaged in lifelong learning and enquiry then we need to provide opportunities to develop these skills in school. We need to nurture a healthy awareness of problems in the world and language surrounding them through study of newspapers and the media. In an increasingly commercialised world, we need to help children to reason, to challenge and to make sense of the barrage of information they are exposed to. We believe that what is essential to literacy is not knowledge but the ability to find out, not just the ability to read and write but to do so with critical understanding, and the skills of reasoned discussion, to help them to question, to communicate and to make a difference for the better.

In creating 'communities of enquiry' in the classroom (as described on p. 7) we develop the skills and dispositions of active citizenship. In particular we need to engage pupils in discussion and consultation about all aspects of school life, as well as engaging them in community action. The school and its local community provide an ideal context for pupils to examine issues and events and for them to become involved in reading and writing for real-life purposes. For example, one primary school which had been running a school council for years, including holding regular 'surgeries' for their constituents, decided to involve the whole school in the production of a school newspaper they called *Fair Comment*. This now has a print run of 6,000 and is distributed throughout the local community. Groups of pupils research articles which they then submit to the editorial team. The paper is funded by advertisements from local businesses, and has the features of a local newspaper including a letters column and comment on local issues. Another school has become involved in the 'Newswise' project, an Internet forum for teachers and pupils based on topical stories adapted from the national press[3]. In another school, children have been involved in a campaign to improve one aspect of their local environment, and wrote letters to local newspapers, the local council, and to the government minister concerned.

Activities such as those we have described aim to unlock more than literacy. They also seek to develop in pupils the capacity to become independent learners and to be active citizens, conscious of their rights and responsibilities. They help to give children the language skills and the confidence they will need to become not only consumers of the culture of the present and the past, but creators of the culture of the future. As Cheryl, aged ten, said, after receiving a reply from the government minister's office to the letter she had sent: 'It was good to write, to share my thoughts and feelings, to try to make the world a better place. Now I'll feel able to do it any time . . .'

Notes

1. See J. Oldham (1999) 'The book of the film: enhancing print literacy at KS3', *English in Education* **33**(1), Spring 1999, 38.
2. The Crick Report is published by DfEE (1998) as *Education for Citizenship and Teaching of Democracy in Schools: Final Report of the Advisory Group on Citizenship*. London: Qualifications and Curriculum Authority.
3. 'Newswise' can be found at http//www.ndirect.co.uk/~sapere/Newswise

Further reading

Buckingham, D. (1999) 'Superhighway on road to nowhere? Children's relationships with digital technology', *English in Education* **33**(1), Spring 1999.

DfEE (1998) *Education for Citizenship and Teaching of Democracy in Schools: Final Report of the Advisory Group on Citizenship*. London: Qualifications and Curriculum Authority.

DfEE (1999) *English in the National Curriculum*. London: HMSO.

Goodwyn, A. (1992) *English Teaching and Media Education*. Milton Keynes: Open University Press.

Oldham, J. (1999) 'The book of the film: enhancing print literacy at KS3', *English in Education* **33**(1), Spring 1999.

Index